2010

WORLD INVESTMENT AND POLITICAL RISK

World Investment Trends
and Corporate Perspectives

Investment and Political Risk
in Conflict-Affected and
Fragile Economies

The Political Risk Insurance Industry

TABLE OF CONTENTS

BOXES

TABLES

FIGURES

FOREWORD

The mission of the Multilateral Investment Guarantee Agency (MIGA) is to promote foreign direct investment (FDI) into developing countries to support economic growth, reduce poverty, and improve people's lives. As part of this mandate, the agency seeks to foster a better understanding of investors' perceptions of political risk as they relate to FDI, as well as the role of the political risk insurance (PRI) industry in mitigating these risks.

The global economy is emerging from a severe recession that slowed down growth and curtailed capital flows to developing countries. FDI was not spared. Having declined sharply in 2009, FDI flows to developing countries are expected to recover in 2010—but in an uneven fashion. Yet, developing countries are projected to grow nearly twice as fast as industrialized countries, enhancing their appeal to multinational enterprises that seek new markets. Corporate views on investment prospects presented in this report not only confirm this appeal, but also highlight persistent investor concerns about a spectrum of political risks.

FDI continues to be concentrated in a handful of countries. Faced with a vicious cycle of conflict and poverty, many of the world's poorest countries are not able to attract sizeable volumes of such investment, putting their prospects for stability and growth into an even more precarious position.

Conflict-affected and fragile economies suffer from cycles of political violence that are hard to break and from a high probability of relapse into conflict. Steady economic growth and rising incomes following conflict can lead to a substantial reduction in the risk of relapse. FDI is an important element in helping to break that vicious cycle by supporting economic growth and development through the transfer of tangible and intangible assets, such as capital, skills, technological innovation, and managerial expertise.

This report focuses on the role that political risk perceptions play in influencing cross-border investment decisions into conflict-affected and fragile economies. Specifically, the report examines (i) the overall trends in FDI and corporate perspectives regarding political risk in the aftermath of the global financial crisis; (ii) the influence that conflict and fragility have on investor political risk perceptions and investment decisions; and (iii) an overview of the PRI industry in the aftermath of the crisis, and how investment insurance providers, especially multilateral organizations, can act as catalysts to help drive FDI into this group of countries.

The global economy is still in flux, but the outlook for FDI is slowly improving. We hope that this report helps shed additional light on how investors perceive and mitigate political risks in conflict-affected and fragile economies, as well as the role that investment insurance providers, including MIGA, can play in fostering such investment.

Izumi Kobayashi
Executive Vice President

ACKNOWLEDGMENTS

This report was prepared by a team led by Daniel Villar and Stephan Dreyhaupt and included Persephone Economou, Gero Verheyen, Caroline Lambert, and Emanuel Salinas. The econometric model presented in chapter 2 was developed by Raphael Reinke. Moritz Zander contributed to the statistical analysis. Research assistance was provided by Thomas Tichar. Caroline Lambert edited the report, and Suzanne Pelland was in charge of graphic design. Melissa Johnson provided administrative support.

The report benefited from guidance and suggestions from the editorial committee led by James Bond, MIGA's Chief Operating Officer. Other committee members were Edith Quintrell, Marcus Williams, Marc Roex, Mallory Saleson, Mansoor Dailami, Jonathan Halpern, and Paola Scalabrin. We also would like to thank current and former MIGA colleagues for their inputs, in particular Nabil Fawaz, Layali Abdeen, Emily Harwit, and Monique Koning.

The World Bank's Development Prospects Group, under the guidance of Andrew Burns, provided the macroeconomic data presented in the report, as well as comments on the analysis. The investor surveys were conducted on behalf of MIGA by the Economist Intelligence Unit. The United Nations Conference on Trade and Development (UNCTAD) contributed information on international investment agreements. The report benefited from invaluable cooperation and inputs from the Berne Union Secretariat, particularly from Lennart Skarp, Deputy Secretary General. The analysis of the political risk insurance market would not have been possible without the gracious participation of political risk insurers in a survey conducted by MIGA and in a roundtable discussion in London organized by Exporta Publishing and Events Ltd. In addition, Gallagher London provided data on the private insurance market. The team also wishes to thank the African Trade Insurance Agency, the Islamic Corporation for Insurance of Investments and Export Credit, and the Office National Du Ducroire for their contributions on conflict-affected and fragile states. Case studies for chapter 2 would not have been possible without the cooperation of SN Power, Statkraft, AngloGold Ashanti, Human Rights Watch, and Old Mutual.

Peer reviews were provided by Andrew Burns (Manager, Development Prospects Group); Dilek Aykut (Senior Economist, Development Prospects Group); the team of the World Bank's World Development Report 2011; James Zhan (Director, Investment and Enterprise, UNCTAD); Juana de Catheu (Team Leader, International Network on Conflict and Fragility, Organisation for Economic Co-operation and Development/OECD); Michael Gestrin (Senior Economist, Investment Division, OECD); Theodore H. Moran (Marcus Wallenberg Chair at the School of Foreign Service, Georgetown University); Desha Girod (Assistant Professor, Department of Government, Georgetown University); and Laza Kekic (Director for Country Forecasting Services, The Economist Intelligence Unit). Additional comments were received from Charles Berry (BPL Global); Toby Heppel (RFIB Group); David Neckar (Willis); Lisa Curtis (DeRisk); Nabila Assaf (Operations Officer at the World Bank's Fragile and Conflict-Affected Countries Group); Joerg Weber (Chief of UNCTAD's International Investment Agreements Section); and Karl P. Sauvant (Executive Director of the Vale Columbia Center on Sustainable International Investment).

SELECTED ABBREVIATIONS

ATI	African Trade Insurance Agency
BU	Berne Union
CAF	Conflict-affected and fragile
DAC	Development Assistance Committee
ECA	Export credit agency
EIU	Economist Intelligence Unit
FDI	Foreign direct investment
GDP	Gross domestic product
ICIEC	Islamic Corporation for Insurance of Investments and Export Credit
ICSID	International Centre for Settlement of Investment Disputes
IDA	International Development Association
IMF	International Monetary Fund
MIGA	Multilateral Investment Guarantee Agency
NGO	Nongovernmental organization
ODA	Official development assistance
OECD	Organisation for Economic Co-operation and Development
OPIC	Overseas Private Investment Corporation
PIF	Palestine Investment Corporation
PRI	Political risk insurance
UNCTAD	United Nations Conference on Trade and Development

Dollars are current U.S. dollars unless otherwise specified.

EXECUTIVE SUMMARY

Political risk remains the top preoccupation for foreign investors operating in developing countries over the next three years, in spite of persistent concerns over the global downturn in the short term. The global economic recession triggered by the financial crisis that has unfolded over the past two years has not spared the developing world. Yet, the fragile and modest recovery now under way is being led by developing countries, which are expected to remain attractive destinations for foreign direct investment (FDI). In light of overt political risk perceptions, the revival of FDI to these destinations calls for continued risk mitigation, including political risk insurance (PRI).

Only a few countries are expected to keep absorbing most FDI flows to the developing world. However, most conflict-affected and fragile (CAF) economies struggle to attract private capital. This is caused not only by the risk of political violence, but also by structural weaknesses. Yet, economic development is an essential component of stability. Together with other types of capital flows, FDI—by providing much-needed financial resources, technology transfer, managerial expertise, and connections to the global economy—can help generate sustained, private-sector-led economic growth, which is a necessary condition for economic development and poverty alleviation. Given the limited availability of skilled human resources in CAF countries, FDI may be one of the critical components supporting this development process, which, in turn, helps prevent a relapse into violent conflict.

Besides examining general FDI and risk perception trends in developing countries, this year's report focuses on CAF economies. It attempts to better understand political risk perceptions and how they influence investment decisions, as well as the role PRI can play in easing the constraints that foreign investors face and in shaping investment decisions.

Although political risk also affects industrialized countries, this report covers developing countries exclusively. Similarly, the focus is on FDI and PRI for long-term investment, rather than on trade insurance or other forms of risk mitigation. Finally, CAF countries were considered as a group. Even though they include heterogeneous economies affected by political violence to varying degrees, it was not always possible to refine the analysis to take these distinctions into account. This report is meant to shed partial light on a broad topic that requires further research.

The main findings of the report can be summarized as follows:

Political risk remains a top obstacle to FDI in developing countries over the medium term.

In the short term, concerns over the fallout from the financial crisis appear to dominate investors' preoccupations. Yet, FDI projections and surveys conducted for this report suggest that investors are cautiously optimistic about prospects for a global economic recovery led by the developing world. As a result, FDI to developing countries is expected to recover over the medium term. Investors from the primary industries, as well as those based in developing countries, appear particularly bullish in their investment intentions. As concerns over the health of the global economy recede, political risk considerations will return to pre-eminence for investors from both developed and developing countries.

Ranking of the most important constraints for FDI in developing countries

Percent of respondents

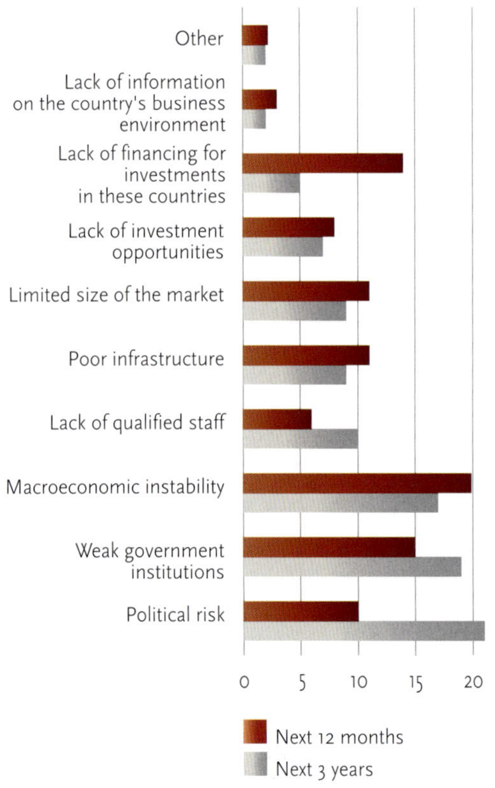

Source: MIGA-EIU Political Risk Survey 2010.

In absolute terms, however, about half the investors surveyed for this report consider that political risk in the developing countries where they operate is not very high, even though a majority reports having suffered losses resulting from these risks.

When considering political perils, corporate decision makers remain most concerned about government interventions that adversely affect the financial viability of their investment, such as changes in regulation, breach of contract, expropriation, and restrictions in currency transfer. This concern confirms results from investor surveys conducted for last year's report.

Conflict and fragility appear to influence FDI through three main channels. As a result, both the composition and role of FDI in CAF economies differ from those observed in other developing countries.

The onset of conflict can affect investment through (i) the possible destruction of assets; (ii) the unavailability of inputs and adequate human resources resulting from the lack of infrastructure and weak institutional and regulatory frameworks; and (iii) abrupt declines in domestic demand, thus leading to lasting impoverishment that persists beyond the end of hostilities. Projects are, therefore, affected to varying degrees depending on sector characteristics, time horizons, and rates of return.

This analytical framework, confirmed in part by econometric analysis and investor surveys, helps explain how FDI flows to CAF economies differ from patterns observed in developing countries. Although the amount of FDI flowing into CAF countries is in line with their global economic weight, it dwarfs other sources of private capital flows such as debt and portfolio investment, which, unlike in other developing countries, are minimal in CAF economies. In addition, FDI flows to CAF countries are heavily dominated by extractive industries.

Investors are primarily concerned about adverse government intervention rather than political violence, even in CAF states.

Respondents operating in CAF and other developing countries alike are more concerned about changes in regulations, non-honoring of sovereign guarantees, currency restrictions, and expropriation than risks of political violence. Changes in regulations not only ranks first among investors' concerns in CAF countries, but also is most frequently responsible for losses in these investment destinations. The risk of civil disturbance, however, is more salient among investors' concerns and more often is responsible for losses in CAF economies than in developing countries in general. The risk of war and terrorism, however, ranks low for both groups.

Political risks of most concern to foreign investors

Percent of respondents

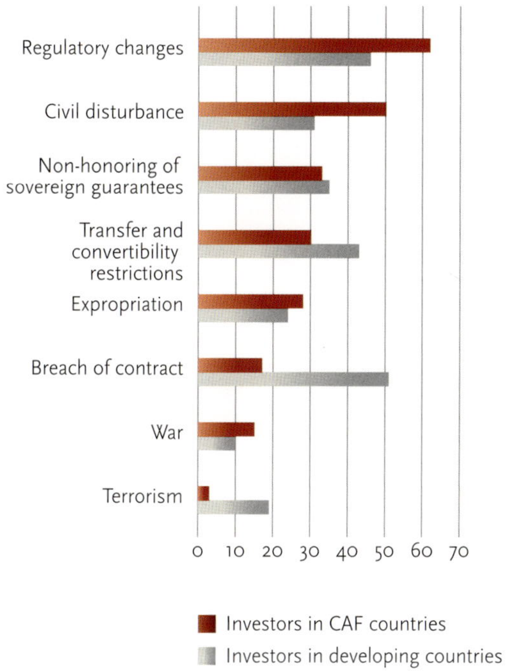

Source: MIGA-EIU Political Risk Survey 2010 and MIGA-EIU CAF Investors Survey.
Note: Percentages add up to more than 100 because of multiple selections.

Foreign investors involved in developing countries use a wide range of risk-mitigation techniques to manage political perils. Yet, PRI remains a niche product, in particular in CAF countries. The main reasons cited for not using insurance in these investment destinations are the limited level of risk and low levels of potential losses, suggesting that investors operating in CAF economies may have a higher tolerance for risk. But this finding may also reflect the PRI industry's shortcomings, because a significant minority of investors surveyed cite either that they are not familiar with this type of insurance, or that what is available is inadequate.

Overall, business opportunities in a predictable regulatory environment appear to override concerns over political peril, even in CAF economies. As a result, the availability of PRI does not appear to weigh significantly on investment decisions for most survey respondents involved in CAF countries. Yet, investors in industries such as financial services are more sensitive to whether they can obtain PRI than are those operating in the primary sector. This finding suggests that, although insurance may not result in much additional FDI to CAF countries, it could potentially help diversify the sector composition of these flows.

Multilateral PRI providers have a key role to play not only in directly covering FDI in CAF countries, but also in mobilizing additional insurance in the market.

Outstanding PRI cover in CAF countries is concentrated in a handful of countries that are well endowed in natural resources and has been underwritten by few insurers. Although a number of export credit agencies are restricted by risk ratings and foreign policy considerations, a few private PRI providers have been active in CAF destinations, but mainly in the extractive and energy sectors, partly reflecting the composition of FDI flows.

Because of their ownership structure and mandates, however, multilateral PRI providers are uniquely positioned to encourage investment in CAF countries, to offer some deterrence against adverse government intervention, and to mediate disputes before they turn into losses. They are, therefore, well placed to encourage coinsurance and reinsurance in investment destinations that other insurers may not have otherwise considered, as demonstrated through a number of initiatives targeting CAF countries.

CHAPTER ONE

WORLD INVESTMENT TRENDS AND CORPORATE PERSPECTIVES

Overview

The world economy is emerging from a severe economic downturn, which has taken its toll on private capital flows, including foreign direct investment (FDI).[1] Showing resilience during the initial phase of the global financial crisis, FDI flows to developing countries[2] then dropped by 40 percent in 2009 on average, although South Asia, the Middle East and North Africa, and sub-Saharan Africa were less affected than were other developing regions. This decline was similar to the trend observed in developed countries. Yet, FDI continues to be the largest source of international private capital in the developing world. A small number of countries absorb the bulk of such investment, however.

As the global economic outlook slowly improves, so do prospects for foreign investment. Developing economies, which are expected to grow twice as fast as the developed world, are expected to have a modest recovery in FDI flows. Investors surveyed for this report remain keen to expand in developing countries, particularly in the medium term. Those from the primary sector, in light of rising commodity prices, appear to be the most bullish, together with investors based in developing countries (South-based investors).

Developments in the global economy have only temporarily overshadowed concerns about political risk. Investors from both developed and developing countries rank political perils as the top constraint to investing in the developing world over the next three years. On the one hand, risks related to government intervention—particularly adverse regulatory changes and breach of contract—are considered the highest and are affecting investors' operations the most. On the other hand, the risk of political violence is perceived to be low relative to other perils and to have the smallest impact.

Even though a majority of surveyed investors report having suffered losses resulting from political risk, about half of respondents do not consider political perils very high in absolute terms in the developing countries where they operate. Only one in three investors currently uses contractual risk-mitigation tools—and only 21 percent turn to political risk insurance, opting instead for a range of informal techniques.

Global Recovery and Economic Prospects

Following an acute recession, the world economy has now entered a phase of recovery, albeit not without risks and with a great deal of turmoil and unevenness. Policy challenges have shifted from preventing a collapse of the private-sector financial system, to dealing with risks posed by fiscal positions of several high-income countries in Europe, and to taking difficult structural steps to ensure that the recovery is sustainable. The interventions that stabilized the international banking system and that softened the impact of the financial crisis on the real economy were achieved at great cost. Public-sector deficits and debt to gross domestic product (GDP) ratios among G7 countries have ballooned to levels that have not been seen since the 1950s. At the same time, the health of financial markets, while much improved, remains fragile. The process of reregulation of financial markets has barely begun, and significant additional consolidation and recapitalization, as well as a return of market confidence and credit demand, are required before banks in high-income countries can be expected to step up lending.

In spite of these challenges, the real economy is rebounding out of the 2009 recession. Global industrial production expanded by 9 percent (annualized rate) in the second quarter of 2010, while merchandise trade increased by 22 percent (annualized rate).[3] Global GDP is expected to grow by 3.3 percent in 2010 and 2011 and to rise to 3.5 percent in 2012 (table 1.1).

Developing economies, sustained by buoyant domestic demand, are expected to grow by at least 6 percent a year in 2010, 2011, and 2012—more than twice as fast as high-income countries. Developing countries are expected to generate close to half the annual increase in global demand between 2010 and 2012, and their rapidly rising imports will also account for more than 30 percent of the increase in global exports.[4] As a result, they are anticipated to be a major driver of global growth over the next few years. The combination of the steep decline in activity in 2009 and the relatively weak recovery projected in the high-income countries, however, means that developing economies are likely to be operating below capacity and that unemployment, although on the decline, will continue to be a serious problem.

Economic growth in China and India, which has been underpinning the recovery in the developing world, appears to be slowing as the impact of the domestic policy stimulus and inventory cycle is waning. Other middle-income developing economies, however, are picking up, thanks to accelerating domestic and global demand. Countries in East Asia and the Pacific benefited from close links to China, where a large government stimulus package boosted investment and growth. Similarly, government intervention to mitigate the impact of the global crisis in the Russian Federation has reverberated across Central and Eastern Europe, where stronger commodity prices and improved global financial stability have also contributed to an uneven recovery. The outlook for the Middle East and Africa will continue to rely on recovering commodity prices and stronger external demand. Latin America's recovery will largely be driven by private consumption as government spending is expected to wane. Overall, prospects for developing countries will increasingly be determined by domestic demand and private-sector activity, by the global trade environment and commodity prices, and by how they address fiscal and longer-term structural challenges.

Capital Flows in the Aftermath of the Crisis

The global crisis resulted in a continued decline in private capital flows and remittances to developing countries in 2009, while official lending and official development assistance (ODA) held up. Aggregate

Table 1.1 The global economic outlook, 2008–2012
Percentage change from previous year

	2008	2009[e]	2010[f]	2011[f]	2012[f]
World	1.7	-2.1	3.3	3.3	3.5
High-income countries	0.4	-3.3	2.3	2.4	2.7
Developing countries	5.7	1.7	6.2	6.0	6.0
East Asia and the Pacific	8.5	7.1	8.7	7.8	7.7
Europe and Central Asia	4.2	-5.3	4.1	4.2	4.5
Latin America and the Caribbean	4.1	-2.3	4.5	4.1	4.2
Middle East and North Africa	4.2	3.2	4.0	4.3	4.5
South Asia	4.9	7.1	7.5	8.0	7.7
Sub-Saharan Africa	5.0	1.6	4.5	5.1	5.4
Memorandum items					
Developing countries					
excluding transition countries	5.7	3.0	6.6	6.2	6.2
excluding China and India	4.3	-1.8	4.5	4.4	4.6

Source: World Bank, Global Economic Prospects 2010 and revised estimates.
Note: e=estimate; f=forecast.

private and official financial flows fell sharply for a second year in a row in 2009, declining by 29 percent to $554 billion (3 percent of GDP), from $778 billion (4.5 percent of GDP) in 2008 (table 1.2). The slump was largely due to declining FDI and the collapse of private debt, which overshadowed recovering portfolio equity flows and a tripling in official lending.

Financial flows to developing countries began strengthening toward the end of 2009, however, and are expected to slowly recover over the medium term, sustained by private capital. Net private flows (which include FDI and portfolio equity flows, as well as debt from private creditors) are projected to rebound in 2010 and 2011, but to remain substantially lower than their $1.2 trillion peak in 2007 (8.5 percent of GDP) (figure 1.1). Although bank lending collapsed, bond issuance and short-term, mostly trade-related debt flows began to rebound as early as 2009. Going forward, however, tighter financial regulations and competition for international funding from high-income countries (when the interest rate environment changes in those markets) are expected to weigh on private capital flows to developing economies.

Relatively immune to the effects of the financial crisis on major donor countries, ODA to developing countries was virtually unchanged in 2009 (figure 1.2). ODA in constant terms reached $123.1 billion in 2009, marginally above the $122.3 billion in 2008. Bilateral ODA declined slightly from $87 billion in 2008 to $86 billion in 2009 in constant terms. However, the nature of ODA did shift, as bilateral concessional loans replaced bilateral grants in 2009, likely reflecting fiscal stress in donor countries.

Figure 1.1 Net private capital flows to developing countries

$ billion and percent

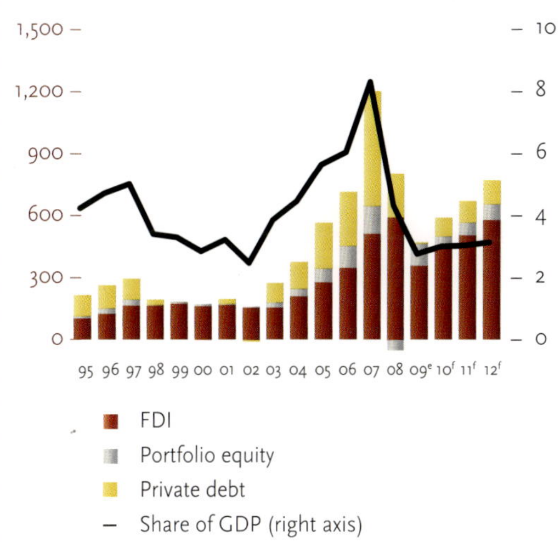

Source: World Bank, Global Economic Prospects 2010 and revised estimates.
Note: e=estimate; f=forecast.

Table 1.2 Net international capital flows to developing countries

$ billion

	2005	2006	2007	2008	2009[e]	2010[f]	2011[f]	2012[f]
Net private and official inflows	493	642	1,202	778	554	–	–	–
Net private inflows (equity + debt)	564	714	1,203	750	470	568	670	771
Net FDI inflows	274	343	508	587	354	416	501	575
Net portfolio equity inflows	67	108	135	-53	108	60	63	78
Net debt flows: official creditors	-71.5	-72.3	-0.9	28.1	83.4	–	–	–
Net debt flows: private creditors	223	263	560	216	8	92	106	118

Source: World Bank, Global Economic Prospects 2010 and revised estimates.
Note: e=estimate; f=forecast; – = not available.

Following a 6 percent decline to $316 billion in 2009, workers' remittances are expected to rebound by 6 percent in 2010 and 7 percent in 2011, supported by the modest recovery in high-income countries. However, continued high unemployment rates, tighter immigration controls, and exchange rate uncertainties will keep affecting remittances.

Figure 1.2 ODA into developing countries

$ billion

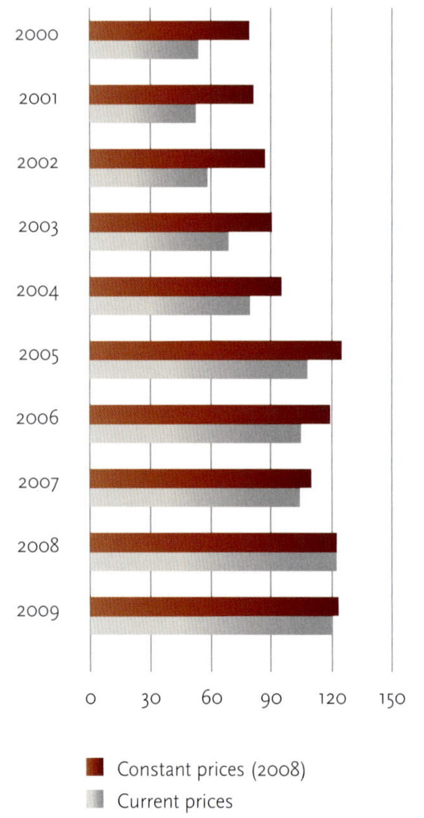

Source: World Bank, Global Economic Prospects 2010.

The Rebound of FDI Flows into Developing Countries

Although FDI flows worldwide are showing signs of recovery in 2010, the rebound was anemic in light of the severity of the recession, especially in the developed world (figure 1.3). Multinational enterprises (MNEs) were hit hard by the global economic recession and financial crisis of 2008. Slower global growth in 2008 and 2009 squeezed their profitability, while global economic uncertainty, weak global demand, and the credit crunch affected their willingness and ability to expand overseas. As a result, global FDI flows declined from $1.8 trillion in 2008 to an estimated $1.1 trillion in 2010—51 percent below the 2007 peak of $2.3 trillion.

Figure 1.3 FDI flows worldwide

$ billion

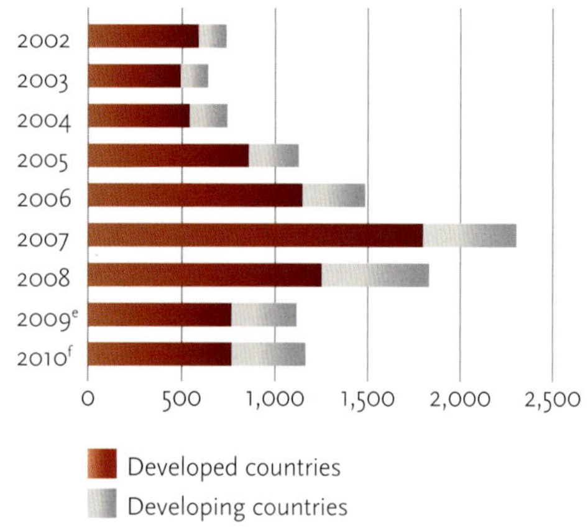

Source: World Bank estimates.
Note: e=estimate; f=forecast.

The developing world absorbed about 37 percent of global FDI flows in 2009—a proportion that has risen over the past decade and is expected to continue expanding, attesting to the growing significance of the flows in the world economy. After appearing resilient at the onset of the global crisis in 2008, FDI inflows to developing countries slumped by 40 percent in 2009—a decline similar to high-income countries'—to $354 billion (2.1 percent of GDP), compared to $587 billion (3.4 percent of GDP) in 2008.

All developing regions suffered, but the decline was uneven. East Asia and the Pacific, Europe and Central Asia, and Latin America and the Caribbean all experienced declines in FDI of more than 40 percent (figure 1.4); the decline in FDI flows to East Asia and the Pacific was steeper than the decline following the Asian crisis of 1998–1999, and China recorded a record 47 percent drop to $78 billion. Less affected, however, were South Asia, sub-Saharan Africa, and the Middle East and North Africa, thanks in part to natural resource investments. Overall, FDI inflows to the developing world continue to be overwhelmingly concentrated in middle-income countries, with Brazil, the Russian Federation, India, and China (BRIC) alone absorbing about half. Although the share of FDI to low-income countries increased slightly in 2009, it remained below 3 percent of investment to all developing economies.

Figure 1.4 FDI flows by developing region

$ billion

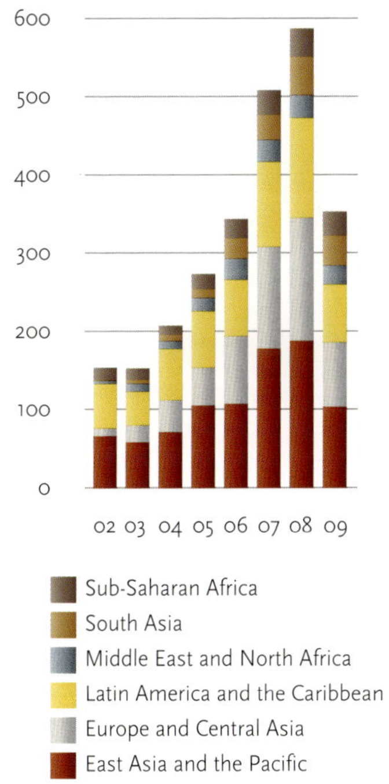

Source: World Bank estimates.

FDI prospects appear brighter for developing countries in 2010 and beyond: their economic performance is expected to outpace that of high-income economies; domestic demand is buoyant, especially in East Asia; high-income countries, a major source of FDI to the developing world, are expected to maintain interest rates low in the short term; and the recovery of commodity prices could encourage higher levels of FDI in the primary sector. Conversely, the global economic recovery remains fragile and uncertain.

Overall, FDI inflows to developing countries are projected to increase by 17 percent to an estimated $416 billion in 2010. They should continue growing by a modest 20 percent and 13 percent a year in 2011 and 2012, respectively, as the global economic recovery strengthens.[5] By 2012, FDI flows to the developing world are expected to reach $575 billion—a figure still below the pre-crisis peak of 2008, thus highlighting the severe impact of the recent downturn.

A survey of 194 executives from MNEs worldwide commissioned by the Multilateral Investment Guarantee Agency (MIGA) in June 2010, the composition of which mirrored that of actual FDI flows by sector and region (the MIGA-EIU Political Risk Survey 2010, see appendix 2) confirms the expected recovery of FDI flows to developing countries in 2010 and beyond. Around 40 percent of those respondents who were surveyed in both 2009 and 2010 expect to increase their investments in developing countries over the next 12 months. That this proportion is not higher than in last year's survey (figure 1.5) suggests that investors remain cash-constrained or cautious, in light of improved but still uncertain prospects for world growth. Yet, investors' measured optimism and improved financial situation is apparent: only 6 percent of respondents in 2010 plan to reduce their investments over the coming year, compared to more than a third of firms surveyed in 2009.

Respondents in both the 2009 and 2010 surveys were more optimistic over the medium term: about two-thirds anticipate to increase their overseas investments, while the proportion of investors expecting to divest from developing countries has more than halved since last year (figure 1.5). This finding is in line with macroeconomic projections, thus suggesting continued FDI recovery over the next couple of years.

Figure 1.5 Changes in foreign investment plans

Percent of respondents

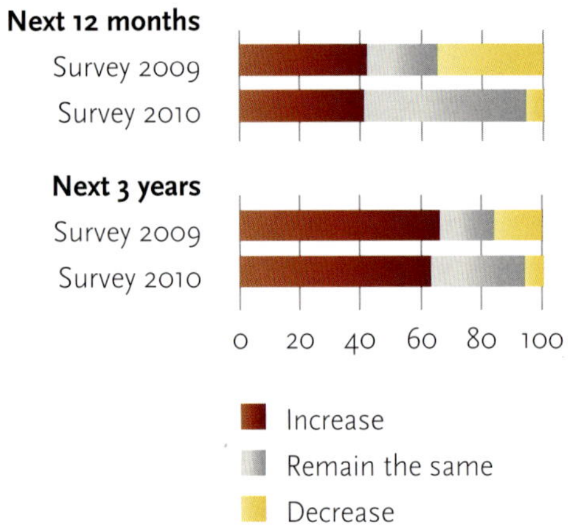

Source: MIGA-EIU Political Risk Survey 2009 and MIGA-EIU Political Risk Survey 2010.
Note: The findings presented here apply only to the group of investors who were surveyed both in 2009 and 2010. Appendix 2 presents the findings for all investors surveyed in 2010.

Unlike the 2009 survey, only a very small proportion of firms surveyed this year plan to decrease their investments in developing countries over the next 12 months, regardless of sectors (figure 1.6). A mixed picture emerges when it comes to increasing investment, however. Respondents from the primary sector appear the most bullish, particularly over the medium term, possibly reflecting the recovery of commodity prices. Firms in telecoms and utilities, conversely, trail other sectors both in the short and medium terms. In addition, only 36 percent of MNEs in the financial sector plan to increase their investment in developing countries in the next 12 months—possibly a reflection of the fallout from the global financial crisis; yet, the proportion almost doubles over the next three years, with two-thirds expecting to expand in developing countries, which suggests expectations of a significant improvement in the business and financial environment.

Figure 1.6 Changes in foreign investment plans by sector

Percent of respondents

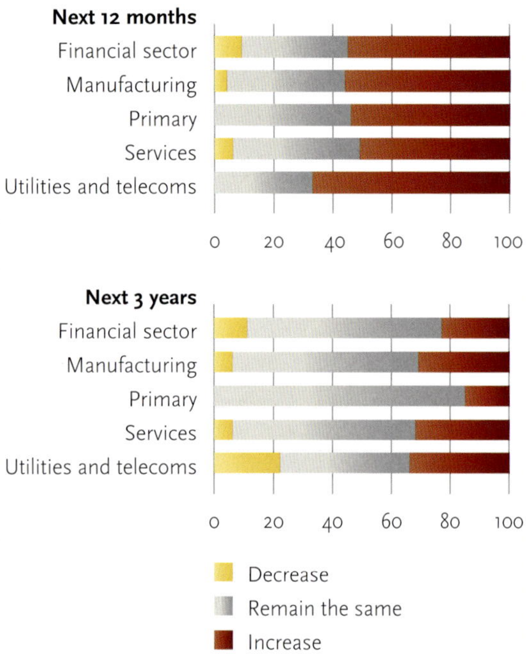

Source: MIGA-EIU Political Risk Survey 2010.

FDI FROM DEVELOPING COUNTRIES

FDI flows originating from developing countries rebounded briskly to an estimated $185 billion in 2010 (figure 1.7). The economic crisis had dampened developing countries' outward investment in 2009, when FDI declined by 28 percent to $149 billion following a record $207 billion in 2008. Much of the slump was attributed to Brazil, where FDI outflows turned negative by $10 billion in 2009 from $20 billion in 2008, as struggling Brazilian companies relied on loans and amortization payments from their foreign affiliates. Despite its severity, that decline was significantly below the drop in FDI flows from developed countries. The relative resilience of developing countries as a source of FDI can be attributed to the growing desire of their MNEs to expand abroad as they seek to access new consumer markets and natural resources. Many of these firms have developed significant brand recognition and a global presence beyond their region. With a limited reliance on international debt markets, the financing of their overseas expansions with cash and domestic debt has helped shield them from the credit crunch.

FDI outflows from the BRIC countries continue to lead. Together they have seen their share of FDI outflows from developing countries increase from 56 percent to 64 percent between the first and second half of the past decade. China and the Russian Federation have been the largest outward investors over the past few years, with $44 billion and $45 billion in FDI outflows in 2009, respectively. Non-BRIC developing countries—notably Chile with $8 billion; Mexico with $7.6 billion in 2009; and even Kazakhstan, whose outward FDI increased three-fold in 2009—are gradually moving up the ranks of outward investors as their MNEs globalize their operations.

Figure 1.7 FDI outflows from developing countries

$ billion and percent

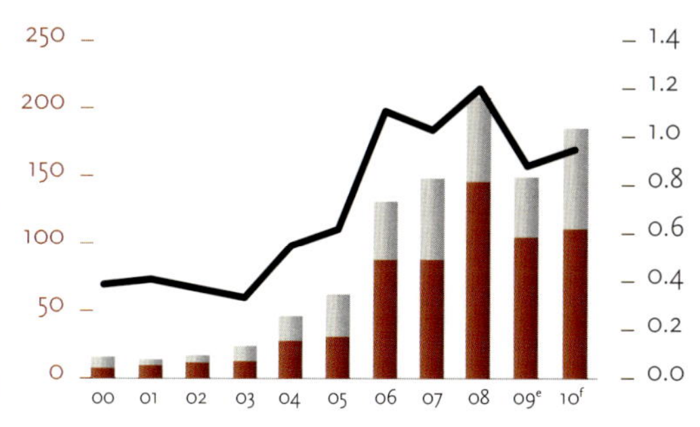

Source: World Bank estimates.
Note: e=estimate; f=forecast.

The MIGA-EIU Political Risk Survey 2010 suggested that the rebound in FDI outflows from developing countries is set to continue. In the short term, respondents based in developing countries are more bullish about investing in the developing world than firms based in high-income countries (figure 1.8). Over the next three years, however, this gap largely closes, with roughly two-thirds of investors from both industrialized and developing economies intending to increase their investments in developing countries. This finding underscores the growing weight of developing countries in the global economy,[6] not only as destinations but also as sources of FDI.

Figure 1.8 Changes in foreign investment plans by source

Percent of respondents

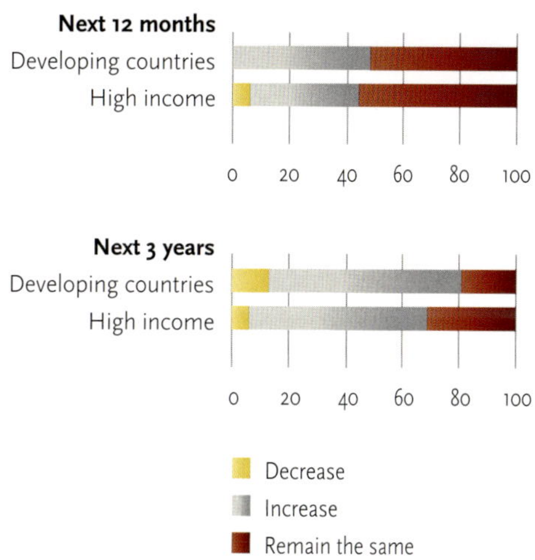

Source: MIGA-EIU Political Risk Survey 2010.

Corporate Perceptions of Political Risk in Developing Countries

Political (or noncommercial) risk facing foreign direct investors is the probability of disruption of MNEs' operations by political forces or events originating in either host countries or home countries, or resulting from changes in the international environment (box 1.1). In host countries, political risk typically refers not only to uncertainty over governments' and political institutions' actions that affect foreign direct investors, but also to dynamics that could result in civil disturbance, terrorism, civil wars, and cross-border conflict. Because of its longer-term nature and assets on the ground, FDI is often more vulnerable to political risk than are other types of cross-border capital flows.

World Investment and Political Risk 2009 highlighted the persistence of investor concerns about political risk in developing countries. Although the link between FDI and political risk is not straightforward, investor surveys carried out in 2009 highlighted that political perils were perceived as a top constraint to cross-border investment by firms based in industrialized countries and developing countries alike. Risks related to government intervention, especially breach of contract, loomed large in investors' perceptions. Restrictions on transfer and convertibility, non-honoring of sovereign guarantees, and civil disturbance ranked high in the short term, but they were expected to recede in the medium term.

These concerns, which predated the recent financial crisis and global economic downturn, have persisted in its aftermath. The MIGA-EIU Political Risk Survey 2010 of MNE executives sought to assess (i) how political risks feature among the factors that constrain investment plans, and (ii) how these risks are being mitigated. How companies perceive, mitigate, and manage these risks needs to be better understood in order to better define the role that PRI can play in this context (chapter 3).

Political Risk: A Major Constraint to FDI in Developing Countries

Developing countries are usually regarded as carrying higher political risk than industrialized countries do, although that notion is increasingly challenged.[7] Although developing economies are still largely moving toward greater investment liberalization and an improvement of the business environment,[8] new limitations on foreign investment and tighter screening and approval processes have been on the rise in recent years. Out of 77 regulatory changes pertaining to FDI introduced by developing countries in 2009, 26 of them introduced restrictions on such investment, the highest share recorded in this decade.[9] Regulatory obstacles specific to FDI and foreign ownership restrictions are more prevalent in select sectors (e.g., media, transportation, and electricity).[10] In addition, the global economic crisis has further exacerbated the debate about the exact role of the state in market economies and state-owned enterprises in FDI[11] that predates the onset of the financial crisis. These developments are likely to weigh on political risk perceptions.

Contributing to investor perceptions of political risk is the increase in the number of treaty-based investment disputes between MNEs and host developing countries, which rose from 23 in 2000 to 206 in 2009. While the increase in the number of disputes is in line with the growth of FDI flows and the promulgation of bilateral investment treaties, defendants in these disputes fall disproportionately in Latin America, with just five countries in that region accounting for 28 percent of all investment treaty claims.[12] This increase is also confirmed by the number of arbitration cases registered with the International Centre for Settlement of Investment Disputes, for which South America alone accounts for 30 percent of all cases.[13]

In response to the recent economic crisis, several developed and developing countries introduced a variety of measures to boost their economies (e.g., economic stimulus packages, state aid, access to finance, or the temporary state acquisition of domestic companies under distress).[14] These measures often aim to protect specific sectors deemed strategic—such as finance or agribusiness—or "national champions." Although most of these measures are meant to be temporary, a revival of state intervention could influence political risk perceptions.

In addition, the global downturn and the measures taken to soften its impact on local economies have resulted in fiscal strains. Although developing countries enjoy stronger public finance and better public debt-to-GDP ratios relative to industrialized countries as they emerge from the crisis,[15] these fiscal pressures, if not managed properly, could undermine governments' ability to meet their financial obligations and local currencies. Although restrictions on the repatriation of profits by foreign investors have so far not materialized, risk perceptions remain high.

Conversely, unwinding rescue packages also carries risks of political instability and civil unrest in some investment destinations if the economic recovery fails to gather enough steam. Removing food subsidies to alleviate ballooning deficits, especially when combined with the recently rising food prices, has resulted in such unrest in a number of developing countries. Food security concerns have also led to large-scale investments involving land acquisitions or long-term land leases, which have sparked civil unrest in several developing countries.[16]

Contract renegotiations in the extractive industry and, in some cases, outright nationalization have contributed to the perceived resurgence of resource nationalism. The decline in the price of many commodities, including oil, from their pre-crisis highs, does not seem to have moderated this risk. A recent survey of mining companies highlights concerns over political instability and security threats.[17] In addition, expropriations and nationalizations in parts of Latin America have spread beyond the extractive industries, into services, public utilities, and manufacturing, thus feeding investors' concerns.

At the same time, some investors argue that new political risks—beyond the traditional concerns surrounding currency convertibility and transfer restriction, political violence, and expropriation—have emerged over the past few years.[18] The rise of local, regional, and nongovernmental interests, including local governments, cultural or religious interests, and nongovernmental organizations (NGOs), has given rise to new uncertainties. Transnational crime and corruption have emerged as political risks affecting foreign firms. In this context, government authorities use their regulatory powers to undermine investor interests. In the worst instances, it is even difficult to separate criminal elements from political interests, because the two are closely aligned. This is especially prevalent in countries with low-transparency, high-corruption indexes or in the so called "failed states."[19] And despite the absence of any major successful attack over the past year, terrorism continues to pose a threat.

In addition, a recent Lloyd's report[20] analyzes the specific political risks arising from the internationalization of production by MNEs, highlighting the interconnectedness of international production and its effect on accelerating the transmission of these risks. The report presents new risks facing globalized production networks, such as supply-chain disruptions caused by political events, with potentially severe impacts on output and the production process. It also underscores how the interconnectedness of production contributes to accelerating the transmission of risks across countries and industries. Finally, it discusses an array of political risks whose presence is not confined to developing countries, such as civil

Box 1.1 What Is Political Risk?

Broadly defined, political risk is the probability of disruption of the operations of multinational enterprises by political forces or events, whether they occur in host countries or result from changes in the international environment. In host countries, political risk is largely determined by uncertainty over the actions not only of governments and political institutions, but also of minority groups such as separatist movements.

For the purposes of the investor surveys conducted for this report, political risk was more specifically defined as a breach of contract by governments; adverse regulatory changes by host countries; restrictions on currency transfer and convertibility; expropriation; political violence (war or civil disturbance such as revolution, insurrection, coup d'état, sabotage, and terrorism); and non-honoring of sovereign guarantees. This definition includes risks that are not currently insurable by the political risk insurance (PRI) industry.

The insurance industry uses a narrower definition of political risk, which usually includes (i) restrictions on currency convertibility and transfer, (ii) expropriation, (iii) political violence, (iv) breach of contract by a host government; and (v) the non-honoring of sovereign financial obligations. Changes in host countries' laws and regulations, however, are not covered. Although there is a general consensus over these broad categories within the PRI industry, exact definitions and labels vary among insurers.

Source: MIGA, *World Investment and Political Risk 2009*.

unrest or the risk of non-honoring of sovereign guarantees, which is closely linked to debt default. The latter is also identified as the second biggest concern in a recent survey of executives by the Economist Intelligence Unit (EIU), after the risk of a "double dip" recession.[21]

Political risk is the single most important constraint for investment into developing countries over the medium term, according to the MIGA-EIU Political Risk Survey 2010. Over the next three years, survey respondents expect to be more constrained by political risk than by macroeconomic instability, limited financing, poor infrastructure, or small market size (figure 1.9). Investors surveyed also rank weak government institutions (including red tape and corruption)—which have a direct bearing on political risk as defined in this report—as the second main constraint to investments into developing countries in the medium term. The growing salience of political risk relative to other concerns over the medium term confirms the findings of the MIGA-EIU Political Risk Survey 2009.[22]

In the short term, however, cross-border investment plans are most significantly hindered by the fallout from the recent financial crisis, the subsequent economic recession, and the persistence of recession-like conditions—even during recovery. Although developing economies rebounded strongly in the first half of 2010, the global recovery has been uneven and remains fraught with risks, as discussed earlier. As a result, macroeconomic instability and lack of financing are at the forefront of investors' concerns when it comes to planned overseas investments in the next 12 months (figure 1.9). Yet, all of these concerns become relatively less prominent over the medium term, suggesting that respondents expect the economic situation to improve.

Firms' expectations that political risk will become the most important constraint for FDI in developing countries in the medium term are consistent across the board. Investors based in developed countries and developing countries alike view political risk as an important constraint to FDI over the next three years. South-based investors view political risk as surpassing all other constraints over the next three years, while weak government institutions, also associated with higher political risk, is their main concern over the next 12 months. The notion that South-based investors might be more tolerant toward political risk because of their familiarity in operating in politically risky domestic environments is not supported by the findings of the MIGA-EIU Political Risk Survey 2010. This was also one of the key findings of the 2009 MIGA-Vale Columbia Center Political Risk Survey in the BRICs.[23] Similarly, there was no substantial difference in the ranking of political risk between small firms and medium or large firms. Both sets of investors viewed political risk as an important constraint in the medium term; medium-size or large firms viewed it slightly more so.

Figure 1.9 Ranking of the most important constraints for FDI in developing countries

Percent of respondents

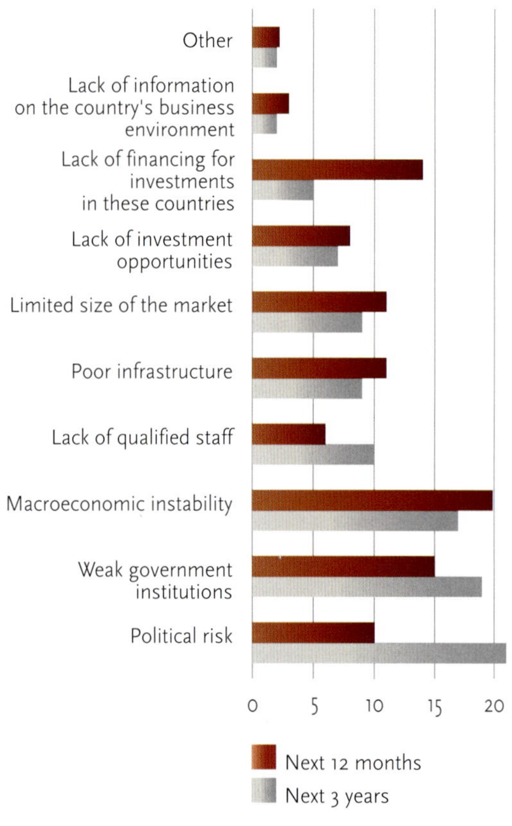

Source: MIGA-EIU Political Risk Survey 2010.

However, there are significant differences in perceptions across sectors. The proportion of firms in the primary sector that found political risk to be the main investment constraint was larger than in any other sector, both in the short and medium terms (figure 1.10). This finding is likely a reflection that investors in that sector—mostly the extractive industries—often operate in difficult and risky environments, with significant sunk costs and long time horizons. Bound by the geography of mineral deposits, they are more constrained in selecting their investment destinations than are investors in other industries.

Figure 1.10 Proportion of firms that identify political risk as the top constraint of FDI in developing countries

Percent of respondents

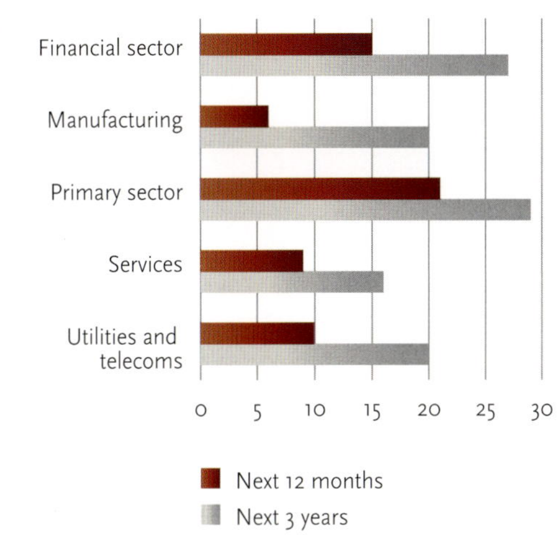

Source: MIGA-EIU Political Risk Survey 2010.

Among various political risks, more investors surveyed are concerned about adverse government interventions—expropriation, restrictions on currency transfer and convertibility, adverse regulatory changes and non-honoring of sovereign guarantees—than about political violence (figure 1.11). Past events influence perceptions of future risks: investors report that most of the losses they have suffered were due to some form of government intervention. In addition, the bulk of FDI to developing countries flows into a handful of developing countries perceived to be relatively stable and to carry a relatively low risk of political violence.

Figure 1.11 Types of political risk of most concern to investors when investing in developing countries

Percent of respondents

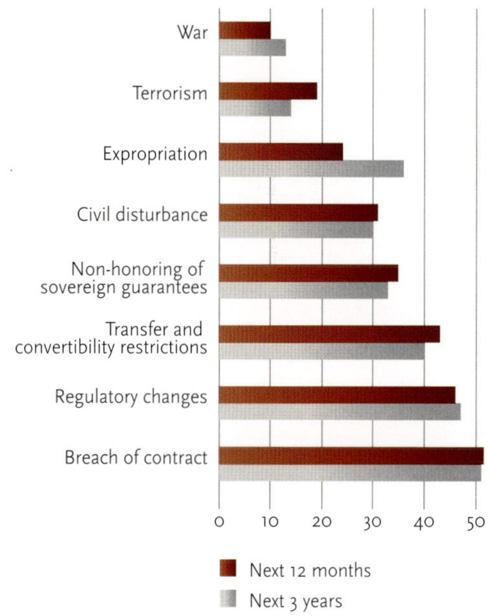

Source: MIGA-EIU Political Risk Survey 2010.
Note: Percentages add up to more than 100 percent because of multiple selections.

Among adverse government interventions, investors are most worried about breach of contract and adverse regulatory changes, both in the short term and over the next three years. There is no significant difference between North- and South-based investors concerning the importance of these two perils, and both had been identified as rising sources of concern by investors surveyed in the MIGA-EIU Political Risk Survey 2009. The risk of transfer and convertibility restrictions, however, is of far greater concern to North- than South-based firms. The latter also appear to be more concerned about civil disturbances. The ranking of perils appears relatively stable over time, with one exception: the proportion of investors citing expropriation rises significantly over the medium term.

Although, as mentioned earlier, the relationship between FDI and political risk is not straightforward,[24] different types of political risk have different bearings on respondents' investment location decisions (figure 1.12). Risks arising from government intervention—in particular breach of contract and adverse regulatory changes—weigh more heavily on these decisions than on those associated with political violence. North-based investors attach greater significance not only to political violence risks than do South-based investors, but also to transfer and convertibility restrictions, with 33 percent of them considering the latter to be of great importance in their investment location decisions.

Figure 1.12 How much importance does your firm assign to each of the risks listed below when deciding on the location of its foreign projects?

Percent of respondents

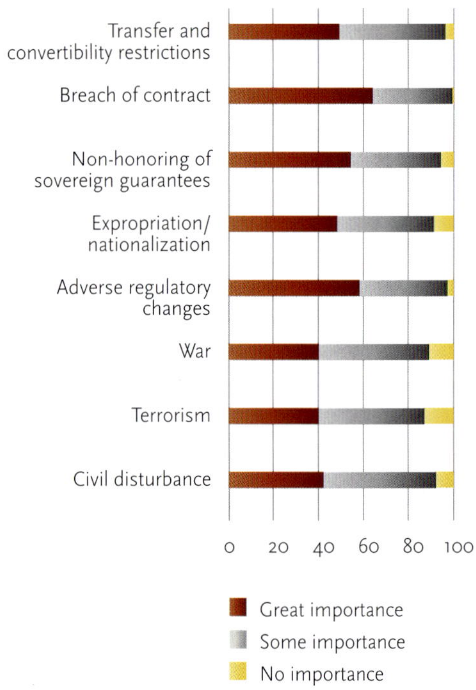

Source: MIGA-EIU Political Risk Survey 2010.

If one follows the rise of resource nationalism over the past few years, it is not surprising that the risk of outright expropriation is of great concern to firms operating in the primary sector (figure 1.13). Firms operating in the telecoms, utilities, and primary industries—whose operations often rely on host government licenses or contracts—are worried mainly about adverse regulatory changes. About twice as many firms in telecoms and utilities, which usually have offtake agreements or guarantees from host governments, are concerned about the willingness and ability of authorities to fulfill their financial obligations, compared to other services. The highest proportion of investors worried about currency transfer restrictions operates in financial services, which often relies on cross-border operations for financing. The risk of political violence—whether civil disturbance, terrorism, or war—is among the lowest across sectors. Mining operations, often isolated and geographically confined, are easier to secure than operations with multiple assets spread across country. At the same time, their sales are not affected by disruptions in local demand that can result from political violence, unlike investments in services targeted at the domestic market.

Figure 1.13 Political risk perceptions in developing countries by type of peril and sector

Percent of respondents

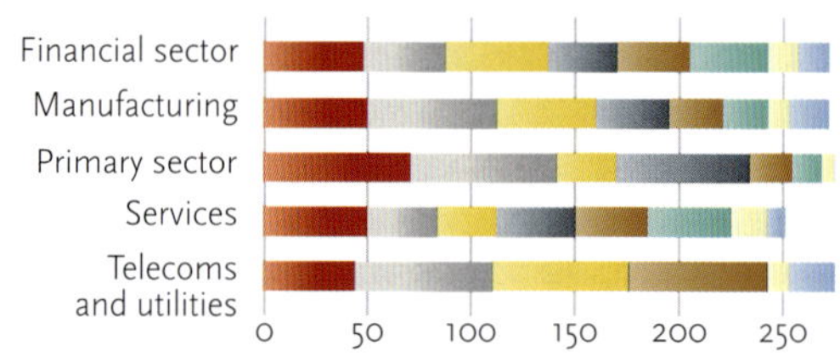

Breach of contract	48	50	71	50	44
Regulatory changes	40	63	71	34	67
Transfer and convertibility restrictions	50	48	29	29	33
Expropriation	33	35	64	38	0
Non-honoring of sovereign guarantees	35	26	21	35	67
Civil disturbance	38	22	14	40	0
Terrorism	15	11	7	18	11
War	15	19	0	9	22

Source: MIGA-EIU Political Risk Survey 2010.
Note: Percentages add up to more than 100 because of multiple selections.

Perceptions of political risks relative to other investment constraints are reflected in investors' views of these risks in absolute terms. Almost half of the investors surveyed (49 percent) consider that the level of risk in one or more categories of political risk in their host developing countries is currently very high (i.e., very likely to occur).

The probability of adverse regulatory changes and breach of contract occurring are perceived to be the highest in the developing countries where these firms are presently investing (figure 1.14). Political violence, conversely, is thought the least likely and to have the smallest impact on operations, reflecting the concentration of the investments in middle-income economies where conflict is largely absent.

Figure 1.14 In the developing countries where your firm invests presently, what is the perceived level for each of the following risks?

Percent of respondents

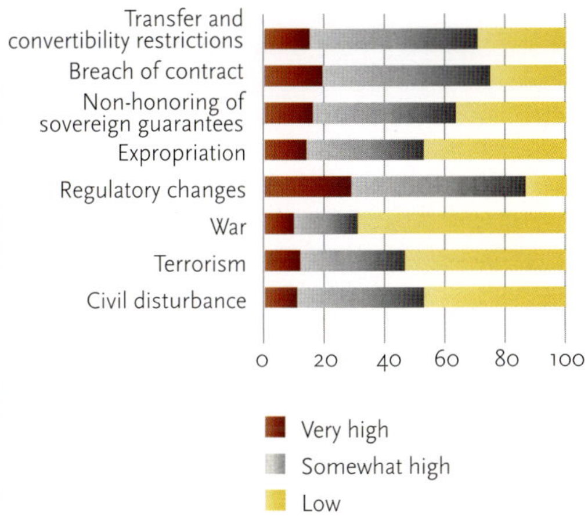

Source: MIGA-EIU Political Risk Survey 2010.

Investors' ranking of the different perils by likelihood of occurrence broadly mirrors their ranking by concern (figure 1.11), with the risk of various types of government intervention perceived to have a higher probability of occurrence than political violence. Yet, the likelihood of perils does not always match the severity of their impact on investment and, therefore, investors' concerns. For example, a perceived high level of risk arising from war and civil unrest implies a greater probability of occurrence of this type of risk, but its actual impact on investment may be small in terms of potential losses. It is both the probability of occurrence for each risk, and the potential losses that each type of risk generates that are likely to influence the choice of risk-mitigation tools.

The occurrence of losses itself appears to have a moderate impact on risk perception. Most respondents do not consider political risks to be very high in their host countries, although some three-quarters of them have experienced losses caused by political risks in one or more of their investment destinations over the past three years. These losses were mostly due to breach of contract and adverse regulatory changes (figure 1.15), both of which are at the top in the list of risks that investors consider high both in absolute terms and relative to other political risks (figure 1.11). Three times as many North-based firms experienced losses related to transfer and convertibility restrictions as did South-based investors. These losses were also more prevalent for medium-size and large firms, as were losses from adverse regulatory changes. Only a small proportion of firms experienced losses owing to political violence, which mirrors the low ranking of these risks in investor concerns.

Figure 1.15 Proportion of firms that have suffered losses caused by political risk over the past three years

Percent of respondents

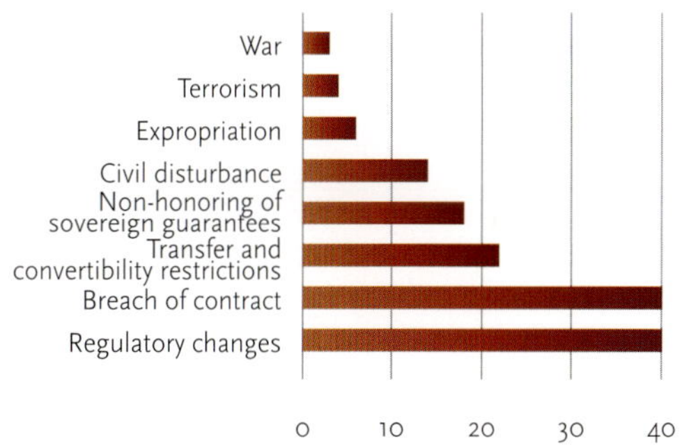

Source: MIGA-EIU Political Risk Survey 2010.
Note: Percentages add up to more than 100 because of multiple selections.

Concerns over expropriation (discussed earlier), however, appear out of line with the frequency of past incidents: although only 6 percent of respondents reported losses due to expropriation, twice as many consider the risk as high. This concern is likely to be related to the potential severity of losses caused by expropriation, which often results in a total loss of investment.

A majority of investors do not view political risk as a reason to cancel a planned investment or withdraw an existing one (figure 1.16). Even political risks that most often caused financial losses and rank high in investors' concerns relative to other perils result only in a minority of respondents reconsidering their investment plans. Political violence, about which most investors appear little concerned, was certainly not perceived to be a reason to withdraw or cancel an existing investment for most respondents.

Figure 1.16 Have any of the following risks caused your company to withdraw an existing investment or cancel planned investments over the past 12 months?

Percent of respondents

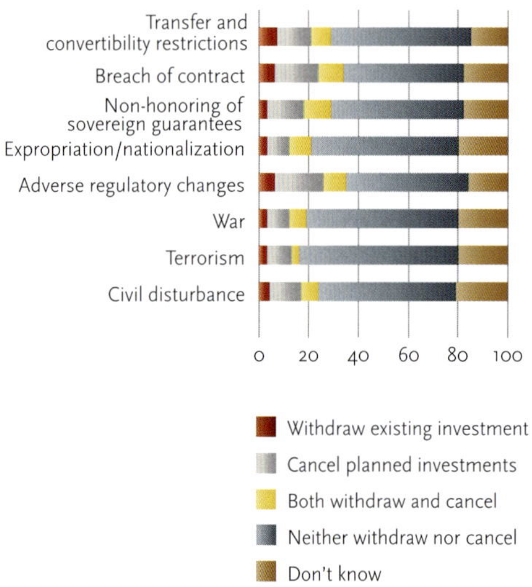

Source: MIGA-EIU Political Risk Survey 2010.

Corporate Approaches to Political Risk Management

The growing salience of political risk relative to other constraints to foreign investment in developing countries, together with survey results suggesting that political risks have caused some losses to a majority of foreign firms involved in those countries, highlight the need to mitigate these risks.

Indeed, the overwhelming majority (95 percent) of investors surveyed for this report actively manage political risk. Risk management includes assessing the level of peril (through internal analysis and the use of consultants); noncontractual mitigation strategies (engagement with local governments, communities, and NGOs, as well as joint ventures with local enterprises and operational hedging); and contractual risk-mitigation tools (such as PRI and credit default swaps).

When it comes to mitigating these risks, the overwhelming majority of investors prefer noncontractual strategies (figure 1.17). Engagement with local governments—such as maintaining an open dialogue and good relationships—and joint ventures with local enterprises were seen as the most effective tools to mitigate the risks of adverse government interventions. Some 63 percent of respondents evaluate and monitor the level of political risk in their investment destinations through internal risk analysis or risk analysis performed by external consultants. South-based investors are slightly more likely to use informal risk-mitigation tools than are North-based investors. Small firms are more likely to engage with local communities and NGOs for risk mitigation than are medium-size and large firms. Investor preference for informal mitigation tools confirms the findings of the MIGA-EIU Political Risk Survey 2009.

Only one in three respondents (32 percent) currently uses contractual risk-mitigation tools, including PRI (21 percent). North-based investors are twice as likely to use PRI compared to South-based investors, despite the fact that both sets of investors are highly concerned about political risk. This limited use may be due to a lack of knowledge about the availability of different PRI products and how they can be used to mitigate risks. Medium-size and large firms are also more likely to use PRI than are smaller firms.

While the proportion of respondents that use PRI is low compared to noncontractual tools, it is significantly higher than the proportion of firms using PRI observed in the MIGA-EIU Political Risk Survey 2009 (14 percent). The increase in the popularity of insurance contrasts with the flat share of FDI to developing countries covered by insurance underwritten by members of the Berne Union in 2009 (see chapter 3).

Figure 1.17 Tools used to mitigate political risk in developing countries

Percent of respondents

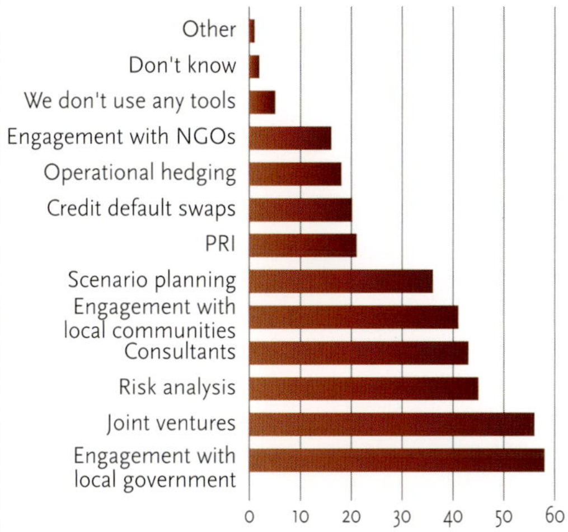

Source: MIGA-EIU Political Risk Survey 2010.
Note: Percentages add to more than 100 because of multiple responses.

Figure 1.18 Most effective tools used to mitigate political risk in developing countries by type of risk

Percent of respondents

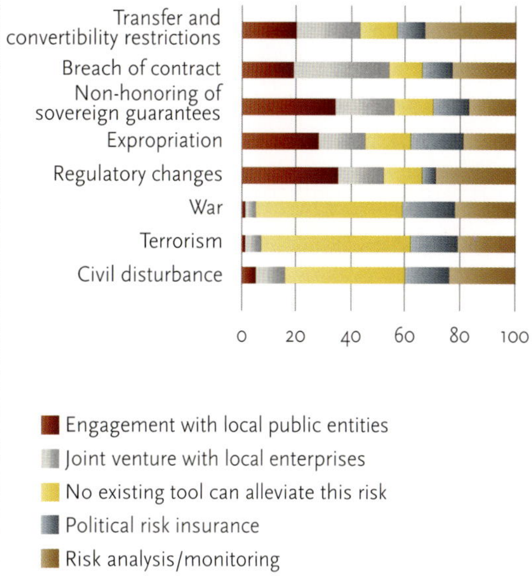

Source: MIGA-EIU Political Risk Survey 2010.

Overall, PRI is regarded as the most effective risk-mitigation tool by 36 percent of investors surveyed.[25] Compared to other risks, PRI was considered relatively more effective for mitigating the risks of expropriation and political violence (figure 1.18). Yet, the proportion of investors who considered that there was no effective mitigation tool against political violence was also significantly higher than for any other risk. The fact that both expropriation and political violence currently rank lower than other perils among investor concerns, as discussed earlier, helps to explain the relatively small role PRI continues to play in risk management, even though it is regarded as being relatively more effective. Yet, it also raises questions about whether there is sufficient awareness among investors of the role PRI can play in mitigating the risks of most concern to investors: only 1 in 10 investors considers PRI as the most effective tool to mitigate breach of contract risk, which ranks highest among investors' concerns (figure 1.18); at the same time, 1 in 20 respondents considers PRI as the most effective way to mitigate the risk of adverse regulatory changes—a peril that is usually difficult to cover by insurance.

Despite concerns about risks and unevenness to economic recovery in the immediate future, investors continue to be optimistic regarding investment plans in developing countries in the medium term. North- and South-based investors remain concerned about political risks as constraints to their overseas investments, and they are more worried about adverse government interventions than political violence. In mitigating risks, most investors turn to informal and noncontractual instruments, with a minority using PRI.

The following chapter examines investment trends and political risk perceptions in conflict-affected and fragile economies.

Chapter One—Endnotes

1 Foreign direct investment is defined as an investment involving a long-term relationship and reflecting a lasting interest and control by a resident entity in one economy in an enterprise that is resident in an economy other than that of the foreign direct investor. It comprises equity investment, reinvested earnings, and intra-company loans.

2 Developing countries are those classified as low- and middle-income countries by the World Bank Group. Developed or industrialized countries are those classified as high income.

3 World Bank, 2010, *Global Economic Prospects 2010*, Washington, DC: World Bank.

4 Ibid.

5 Modest increases are also projected by the Institute of International Finance, 2010, *Capital Flows to Emerging Market Economies*, Washington, DC: IIF and A. T. Kearney, 2010, *Investing in a Rebound: The 2010 A. T. Kearney FDI Confidence Index*. Vienna, VA: A. T. Kearney.

6 OECD, 2010, *Perspectives on Global Development: Shifting Wealth*, Paris: OECD. According to this report, longer-term forecasts suggest that developing countries are likely to account for nearly 60 percent of world GDP by 2030.

7 See Peter Apps, "'Political risk everywhere' Here to Stay," Reuters, June 24, 2010, which also looks at political risk in industrialized countries.

8 World Bank, 2010, *Doing Business 2011: Making a Difference for Entrepreneurs*, Washington, DC: World Bank.

9 United Nations Conference on Trade and Development (UNCTAD), unpublished data. UNCTAD's definition of developing countries differs somewhat from the one used by the World Bank. See also Karl P. Sauvant, 2009, "Driving and Countervailing Forces: A Rebalancing of National FDI Policies," in Karl P. Sauvant, ed., *Yearbook on International Investment Law & Policy 2008–2009*, New York: Oxford University Press.

10 World Bank, 2010, *Investing Across Borders 2010*, Washington, DC: World Bank.

11 Ian Bremmer and Nouriel Roubini, 2010, "Paradise Lost: Why Fallen Markets Will Never Be the Same," *Institutional Investor*, September.

12 UNCTAD, 2010, "Latest Developments in Investor–State Dispute Settlement," IIA Issues Note No. 1, Geneva: UNCTAD.

13 International Centre for Settlement of Investment Disputes (ICSID), 2010, *The ICSID Caseload Statistics*, Issue 2, 2010.

14 OECD and UNCTAD, 2010, *Third Report on G-20 Investment Measures*, June 14, 2010, Geneva: UNCTAD.

15 International Monetary Fund (IMF), 2010, *Fiscal Monitor November 2010*, Washington, DC: IMF.

16 Food and Agriculture Organization, 2009, "From Land Grab to Win-Win," *Policy Brief*, 4, June.

17 Fraser Institute, 2010. *Survey of Mining Companies 2009–2010: 2010 Mid-Year Update*, Toronto: Fraser Institute.

18 Patrick Garver, 2009, "The Changing Face of Political Risk," in Kevin Lu, Gero Verheyen, and Srilal M. Perera, eds., *Investing with Confidence*, Washington, DC: World Bank.

19 Foreign Policy, *The Failed States Index 2010*. http://www.foreignpolicy.com/articles/2010/06/21/2010_failed_states_index_interactive_map_and_rankings.

20 Lloyd's 360 Risk Insight, 2010, *Globalisation and Risks for Business: Implications of an Increasingly Interconnected World*, London: Lloyd's.

21 EIU, "Double-Dip Recession Tops Executives' Concerns for Global Economic Outlook," press release of July 26, 2010.

22 MIGA, 2009, *World Investment and Political Risk 2009*, Washington, DC: World Bank.

23 See findings in ibid.

24 For a review of the literature on FDI and political risk, see MIGA, 2009, ibid., annex 5.

25 This is the proportion of investors that selected PRI as the most effective tool for one or more political risk categories.

CHAPTER TWO

INVESTMENT AND POLITICAL RISK IN CONFLICT-AFFECTED AND FRAGILE ECONOMIES

Overview

Countries considered fragile and prone to conflict present unique challenges, caused not only by heightened risks of new or recurring political violence, but also by structural and institutional weaknesses. As a result, the volume and composition of foreign capital flows to these countries is significantly different from patterns observed in developing countries in general. The econometric analysis presented in this chapter suggests that conflict has a profound negative effect on the number of foreign direct investment (FDI) projects and, even more significantly, on their value. FDI accounts for the bulk of private capital flows to conflict-affected and fragile (CAF) countries because private debt and portfolio investment flows are minimal. FDI in CAF countries is heavily concentrated in a handful of economies, which are either middle income or rich in natural resources. Why some investors in the primary sector opt to invest and others do not, given similar risk perceptions, remains unclear.

In a context of conflict, investment decisions appear to be influenced to a large degree by the risk of asset destruction, of unavailability of local inputs and infrastructure, and of abrupt declines in domestic demand. Investors' relative vulnerability to each of these channels helps explain the sector composition of FDI flows to CAF countries. This analytical framework provides only partial answers. Sectors such as extractive industries and telecommunications—typically large FDI recipients in CAF economies—appear to be outliers when it comes to investor behavior. This finding suggests that other investment considerations, such as geological constraints, the potential for high returns on investment, payback periods, and the ability to mitigate political risk, also weigh heavily on investment decisions.

While the risk of civil disturbance is ranked higher in CAF economies than in developing countries in general, investors are more concerned about the risk of adverse government interventions—regulatory changes, non-honoring of sovereign guarantees, currency restrictions, expropriation, and breach of contract—than about political violence, such as civil disturbance, war, and terrorism. This concern reflects the close correlation between structural and institutional weaknesses and conflict in these countries.

Conflict-Affected and Fragile Economies

There is no single definition of CAF states. For the purpose of this report, CAF economies include the group of countries and territories identified by the political risk insurance (PRI) industry as carrying the highest risk of political violence as of January 1, 2010 (see appendix 3). Among these economies, 18 are considered economically dependent on natural resources.[1] This group overlaps partly with the low-income countries and territories identified by the World Bank as fragile and needing special assistance, according to (i) the World Bank's Country Policy and Institutional Assessment (CPIA) index,[2] or (ii) the presence of a United Nations or a regional peacekeeping or peace-building mission or both during the past three years.

Conflict—defined as a violent "clash between two opposing groups"[3]—has followed diverging trends in recent years; while interstate violence has declined, internal conflict (e.g., civil wars, separatist tensions, and terrorism) has been on the rise. In all cases, conflict is inversely correlated with per capita incomes, and low-income countries are more at risk of violence.[4] According to the World Bank, poverty affects 54 percent of people living in CAF states, compared to 22 percent in low-income countries as a whole.[5] While violence often breeds poverty, the link between low income and conflict goes both ways. Some evidence suggests that worsening economic circumstances, economic shocks, or natural catastrophes can foster political violence.[6] This evidence also applies to the subnational level, with poorer regions within a country being more prone to conflict than wealthier ones.[7]

According to the World Bank's forthcoming *World Development Report 2011*, conflict and fragility are also closely correlated, with fragility indicating a high risk of new conflict or of recurring violence. CAF investment destinations face challenges that not only are limited to conflict per se, but also include weak or non-existent state institutions, inadequate infrastructure, disruptions to supply chains, demand shocks, and difficulty obtaining private debt financing. In countries experiencing conflict or fragility, the economic performance and the ability to deliver basic social services are weak, reflecting poor policies and institutions. In addition, during periods of intense conflict, these economies tend to receive considerably less external assistance than other low-income countries, and their relations with the international financial community are often complicated by high levels of debt and protracted arrears. Some of these constraints are supported by the findings of the surveys commissioned by the Multilateral Investment Guarantee Agency (MIGA) and are cited in this chapter.

A reduction in conflict and a return to political stability often result in improved economic performance. Conversely, economic growth and development are essential to reduce the risk of conflict. By one estimate, a doubling of per capita income roughly halves the risk of civil war, and each point improvement in the CPIA index increases the economic growth rate by 1.25 percentage points.[8] Fostering a virtuous cycle of reconciliation and economic development once violence has broken out is particularly challenging. Some 40 percent of countries coming out of conflict relapse into fighting within 10 years,[9] and around half of all civil wars are due to postconflict relapses.[10] Besides being prone to conflict and instability at home, CAF countries can also destabilize entire regions through refugee flows and barriers to trade and investment.

Foreign capital can contribute to economic growth and development and, therefore, ease fragility and the risk of conflict. Not only can foreign investment increase these countries' productive capacity and generate employment, but also it has the potential to promote the dissemination of managerial and technological expertise that contributes to local firms' improved productivity and competitiveness. It can also generate positive spillovers by fostering local supplier sales and can provide access to international markets.

This chapter seeks to understand the drivers and characteristics of FDI in CAF economies, as well as how investors perceive and mitigate political risk in these destinations.

Table 2.1 Capital flows to CAF economies

$ million

	2005	2006	2007	2008	2009[e]	2010[f]
Net private and official inflows	17,283	32,514	38,861	31,909	33,313	–
Net private inflows (equity + debt)	16,719	30,951	37,045	26,967	24,905	-
Net FDI inflows	14,909	26,353	30,207	28,828	25,192	28,971
Net portfolio equity inflows	1,230	3,035	2,734	(1,104)	5	–
Net debt flows: Official creditors	564	1,563	1,816	4,942	8,408	–
Net debt flows: Private creditors	580	1,563	4,105	(757)	(292)	–
Official development assistance (OECD Development Assistance Committee)	39,768	32,597	24,664	27,577	–	–
Worker remittances	16,894	21,340	28,767	34,129	34,076	–

Source: World Bank estimates.
Note: e=estimate; f=forecast; –=not available.

Capital Flows and FDI Trends in CAF Economies

Because of the challenges outlined earlier, the nature of capital flows to CAF economies diverge from those observed in developing countries in general, where private financial flows—and FDI in particular—constitute the main source of foreign capital (chapter 1). In CAF economies, workers' remittances have become the main source of foreign capital since 2008, overshadowing foreign aid and FDI (table 2.1). These economies also rely more heavily on foreign aid than do other developing countries.

Although foreign aid and international private investment are significant sources of capital flows to CAF countries, their timing tends to be different. Foreign aid, mostly grants, typically make up the bulk of foreign capital in the few years immediately following a period of conflict (figure 2.1). According to the Organisation for Economic Co-operation and Development (OECD),[11] most aid flows to countries as soon as conflict ceases but falls off in subsequent years, just as management capacity to administer aid improves. Private investment, however, picks up when foreign aid flows begin to wane. Remarkably absent in this picture are private debt flows, which shy away from most CAF economies in light of the perceived risk and structural weaknesses that often include weak financial systems.

Figure 2.1 Timeline of foreign aid and investment flows in postconflict states

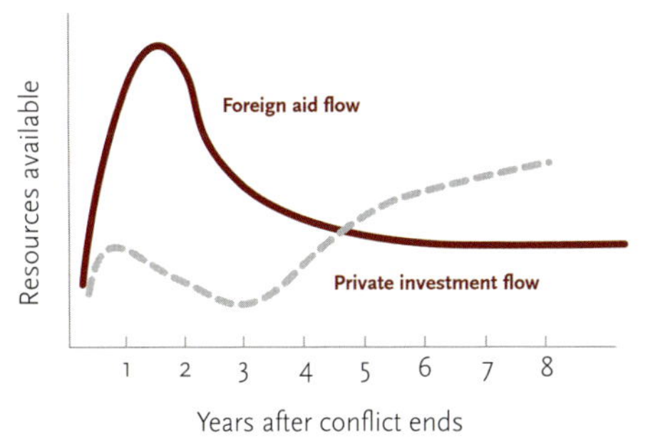

Source: Harry Blair and Katarina Ammitziboell, 2007, *First Steps in Post-Conflict State Building: a UNDP-USAID Study*, Washington, DC: USAID, drawing on Paul Collier, et al, 2003, *Breaking the Conflict Trap: Civil War and Development Policy*, Washington, DC and Oxford: World Bank and Oxford University Press.

Remittances

Worker remittances constitute a financial lifeline for CAF economies, as they do for most countries with low gross domestic product (GDP) per capita. They have been growing rapidly over the past decade, more than doubling in nominal terms between 2005 and 2009 and holding steady in 2009—when FDI flows to CAF countries declined. Remittances account for a higher share of CAF countries' economy than in developing countries (figure 2.2) and have exceeded cumulative FDI flows by nearly $10 billion during 2005–2009 (this figure does not control for GDP per capita because the intention is simply to illustrate the size of flows to CAF countries).

Figure 2.2 Ratio of worker remittances to GDP in CAF and developing countries

Percent

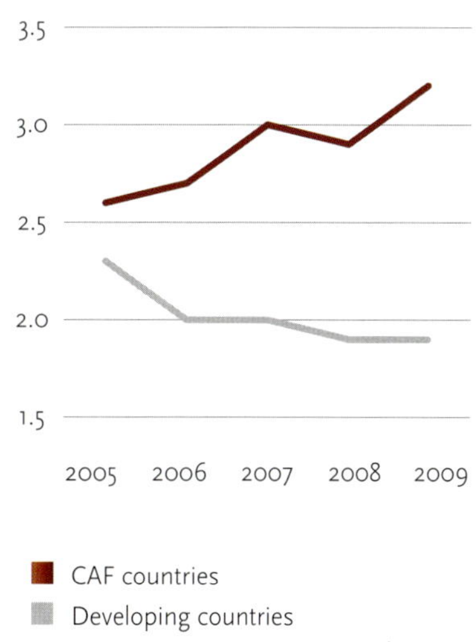

Source: World Bank estimates.

CAF countries absorbed an estimated 11 percent of the $316 billion[12] of worker remittances that flowed into all developing countries in 2009—a significantly higher share than their relative economic weight of 6.3 percent. Although the global economic downturn translated into a 6 percent decline in remittances to developing countries in 2009 (from $336 billion in

2008), these flows held up better in CAF countries. With improved prospects for the global economy, remittances to developing countries are expected to increase by 6 percent in 2010 and 7 percent in 2011, and they should continue to be a key source of foreign capital to CAF economies.

Foreign Assistance

Foreign assistance also constitutes a significant source of external financing for CAF countries, and cumulative official development assistance (ODA) flows to CAF countries were on average 24 percent higher than FDI flows during 2005–2008 (table 2.1). During 2005–2008, CAF countries received 28 percent of cumulative ODA flows from the OECD's Development Assistance Committee (DAC), and this assistance accounted for a higher share of their economies than in developing countries in general (figure 2.3).

Figure 2.3 Ratio of ODA to GDP in CAF and developing countries

Percent

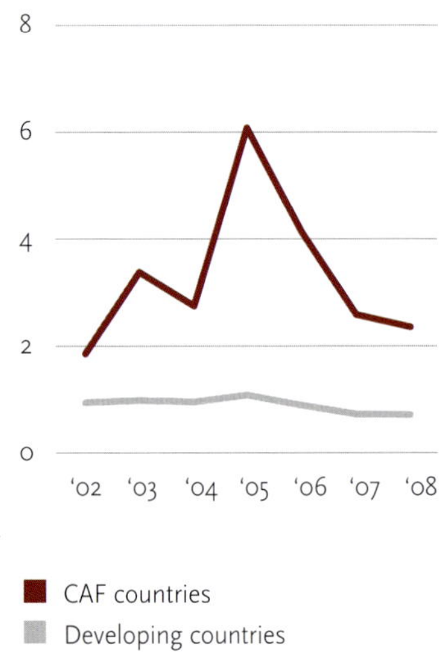

Source: World Bank estimates based on OECD DAC data.
Note: ODA flows from members of the OECD's DAC.

CAF countries also rely on aid from donor countries that are not members of the OECD's DAC (such as China, the Republic of Korea, Saudi Arabia, and Turkey), as well as from global funds and private foundations. Aid from these donors has been growing rapidly. Bilateral aid to fragile states[13] from the limited number of non-DAC donor countries[14] that release data to the OECD is reported to have increased by 68 percent between 2004 and 2008.[15]

Aid to CAF economies from both the OECD's DAC members and non-DAC donors, however, is heavily concentrated. Afghanistan and Iraq account for nearly half of all DAC assistance received by CAF economies during 2005–2008, with Iraq alone absorbing about 40 percent. The doubling of DAC aid flows to CAF countries between 2004 and 2005 was due to a nearly fivefold increase in aid to Iraq. Similarly, four countries (including Afghanistan, Iraq, and Sudan) accounted for almost three-quarters of emerging donors' aid flows to fragile states in 2004–2008. In addition, some fragile states are overwhelmingly dependent on one or two donors for the bulk of the foreign aid they receive.

Official credit to CAF countries is small in absolute value ($17 billion accumulated during 2005–2009) and in relation to both ODA and FDI. Although official debt has more than quadrupled over the past two years (table 2.1), the trend is due to increased lending to a single country. New official debt is heavily concentrated in very few CAF countries, and official credit flows to some CAF economies is actually negative. In addition, most of these countries, especially those without natural resources, struggle to mobilize debt financing. On an aggregate level, the bulk of CAF countries' borrowing is now official credit, especially because foreign private lending has collapsed and even turned negative since the onset of the financial crisis (table 2.1).

CAF economies' external debt stock has historically been high in relation to both the size of their economies and vis-à-vis other developing countries. In each year between 2000 and 2003, their debt to gross national income ratio exceeded 40 percent, compared to roughly 30 percent for developing countries.[16] Although debt flows to CAF countries are usually relatively small, arrears tend to accumulate during periods of conflict and result in fast-ballooning debt obligations.

By 2009, however, debt relief and arrears clearance had contributed to a convergence of the debt to gross national income ratio of around 17 percent for both CAF and developing countries. Debt relief initiatives available to CAF economies include the Heavily Indebted Poor Countries (HIPC) Initiative, the Multilateral Debt Relief Initiative (MDRI), and the administration of the Debt Reduction Facility (for International Development Association [IDA]-only countries). The HIPC Initiative seeks to reduce debt to selected countries that are pursuing adjustment and reform programs, and to countries that are graduating from the process benefit from a 100-percent relief on eligible debt from major multilateral creditors. As of July 2010, 11 CAF states had reached the postcompletion point under this initiative, meaning that creditors have provided irrevocably debt relief. Bilateral debt is also worked out through the Paris Club, which provides exceptional treatment such as deferral of all debt service payments for a specified number of years for CAF states affected by long-standing internal political conflicts.

Foreign Direct Investment

In light of the structural weaknesses outlined in the previous section, most CAF economies struggle to attract substantial foreign investment. In aggregate terms, CAF countries have absorbed between 5 and 8 percent of FDI into developing countries over the past half decade. This small share is broadly in line with their economic weight of 6–7 percent of developing countries' GDP over the same period.

Aggregate FDI flows into CAF countries have largely followed global trends. They increased during the second half of the past decade, reaching a record $30 billion in 2007 (table 2.1) and declined by 5 and 13 percent in 2008 and 2009, respectively, on account of the global economic crisis. In relative terms, the decline of FDI to CAF countries was on average less pronounced than the 40 percent reduction observed in developing countries overall (chapter 1), reflecting the relative resilience of foreign investment in resource-rich economies.

As observed in developing countries in general (chapter 1), FDI flows into CAF countries are heavily concentrated in a few countries. During 2006–2009, the five largest recipients accounted for 60 percent of FDI flows to CAF countries, compared to 54 percent for all developing countries. Low-income countries, conversely, attracted only 15 percent of FDI inflows to CAF economies during 2005–2009.[17] FDI to CAF economies has flowed primarily into resource-rich countries (figure 2.4). These economies accounted for 72 percent of inflows during 2005–2009 on average and for as much as 90 percent in select years.

Figure 2.4 FDI flows into CAF countries

$ billion and percent

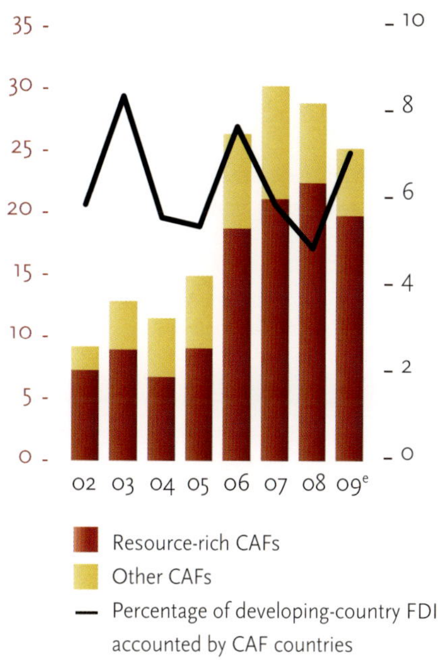

Source: World Bank estimates.
Note: e=estimate.

Sub-Saharan Africa—which accounts for 23 out of 43 CAF economies and most of the 18 resource-rich ones—absorbs more than two-fifths of FDI flows into CAF states. The United States is the largest source of foreign investment into economies, with a stock of FDI valued at around $11 billion as of 2008 (0.4 percent of its global outward stock).[18] China's FDI stock in CAF states stood at roughly $5 billion in 2008 (or 9 percent of its global outward stock).[19]

CAF countries' regulatory framework applicable to FDI is diverse. Although all countries are open to FDI, a number of them restrict foreign ownership in individual sectors.[20] At the same time, CAF countries had concluded 450 bilateral investment treaties (BITs) protecting FDI[21] as of June 2010 (appendix 4). Their share in the universe of BITs exceeds their relative importance in FDI. Just over half of these treaties were with developing countries and the remainder, with developed ones.[22]

Economic and business reform has been essential in attracting FDI into CAF states, in particular in the aftermath of conflict. In the 1990s, Croatia and Mozambique,[23] for example, both implemented significant privatization programs at the end of their respective conflicts, laying the ground for FDI inflows.[24] Yet, while several CAF economies have successfully implemented privatization programs to attract foreign investment and to stimulate the private sector, overall results have been mixed.[25]

Figure 2.5 Private capital flows into CAF and developing countries, cumulative 2005–2009

$ million

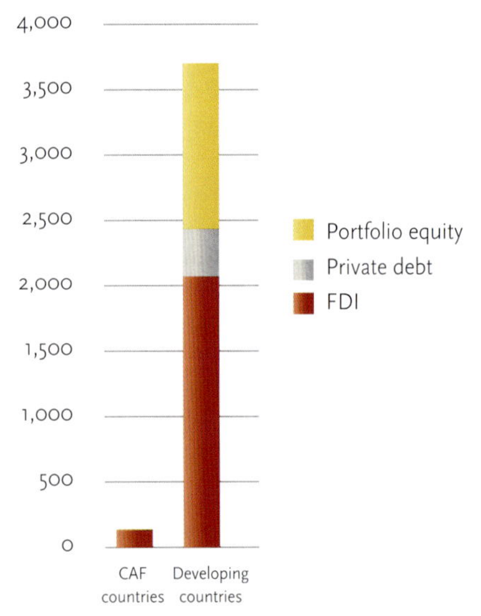

Source: World Bank estimates.

In spite of the small proportion of FDI they attract compared to other developing countries, CAF economies heavily depend on FDI as a source of foreign private capital (figure 2.5). With very limited access to private debt markets, FDI flows exceeded private debt by a factor of 24 during 2005–2009—compared to around two-thirds for developing countries overall (table 2.1 and chapter 1). The dearth of foreign private credit largely limits projects for CAF economies to those that are financed through equity or are assisted by foreign donors. In addition, portfolio equity flows in CAF states are virtually non-existent apart from occasional spikes, largely reflecting the weakness of these economies' financial systems.

Although FDI flows in developing countries dwarf those in CAF states, they account for a similar share of their economies on average (figure 2.6). The aggregate masks substantial variations. The ratio of FDI flows to GDP in some countries[26] can be significantly higher than the average, often exceeding 10 percent. CAF economies not endowed with natural resources tend to rely more heavily on FDI than others.

Figure 2.6 Ratio of FDI to GDP in CAF and developing countries

Percent

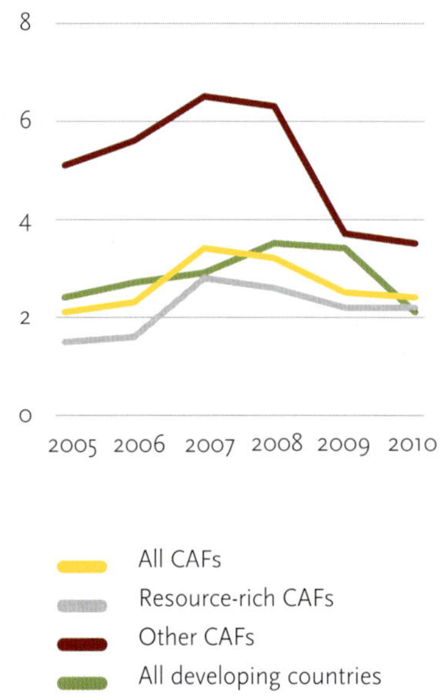

Source: World Bank estimates.

FDI flows, conversely, account for a higher share of gross capital formation in CAF states than in developing countries in general (figure 2.7). This finding reflects low levels of capital formation and the depletion of inventories taking place during periods of conflict, as well as the weakness of local investment in most CAF economies. The gap has broadened since the onset of the global downturn, reflecting the relative resilience of FDI flows to CAF countries compared to developing ones. As mentioned earlier, a significant portion of these aggregate flows are invested in the extractives industries, and investment projects in that sector usually have operational durations that last for decades. Therefore, they suffer less acute fluctuations of flows on a year-by-year basis.

Figure 2.7 Ratio of FDI to gross capital formation in CAF and developing countries

Percent

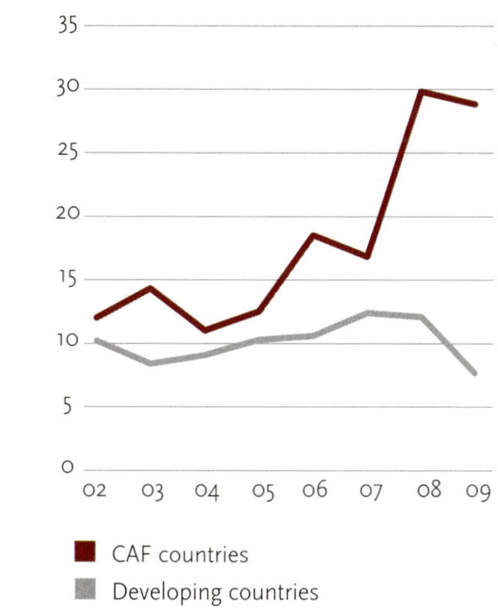

Source: World Bank estimates.

The outlook for foreign investment in CAF countries is expected to improve as the global economy and FDI to developing countries show signs of recovery. These economies are not expected to increase their share of FDI. However, their combined FDI inflows are projected to reach $29 billion in 2010—or 7 percent of flows to all developing countries—up from $25 billion in 2009.[27]

Investor surveys conducted on behalf of MIGA for this report support the general FDI outlook for CAF countries. In addition to the MIGA-EIU Political Risk Survey 2010, MIGA commissioned a survey of investors already involved in CAF countries (the MIGA-EIU CAF Investors Survey) representing 60 multinational enterprises (MNEs) with investments in at least one CAF country conducted in July 2010 (appendix 6). The overwhelming majority of responses from the MIGA-EIU CAF Investors Survey, which indicated intentions to maintain or increase their investments over the next 12 months, showed a small proportion intending to decrease their financial involvement (figure 2.8).

Figure 2.8 Investment intentions of investors operating in CAF countries

Percent of responses

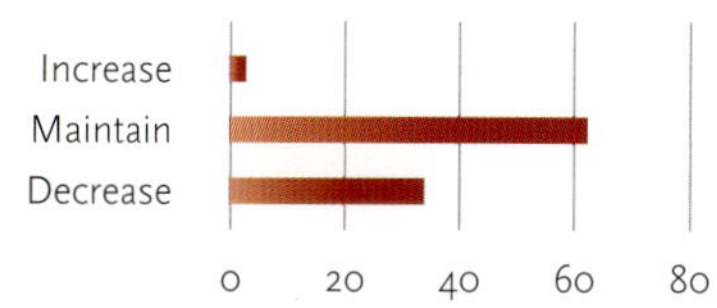

Source: MIGA-EIU CAF Investors Survey.

In addition, almost 40 percent of all respondents in the MIGA-EIU Political Risk Survey 2010 intend to invest in at least one CAF country within the next three years, a slightly higher proportion than those already operating in these countries. The CAF destinations where the largest proportion of MNEs intends to invest are generally middle income or rich in natural resources (figure 2.9), confirming past FDI patterns in this group of countries.

The proportion of respondents operating in the primary sector (57 percent) that intended to invest in CAF economies over the medium term was significantly higher than in other sectors. Continued interest from extractive industries in those investment destinations reflects the global geography of mineral deposits, as well as long investment horizons. That these MNEs have limited choices in their investment destinations compared to other sectors impacts their attitude to political risk, as well as the way they manage it, as outlined in the following section.

Figure 2.9 Top 15 investment destinations among the countries in the top two political violence categories over the next three years

Percent of respondents

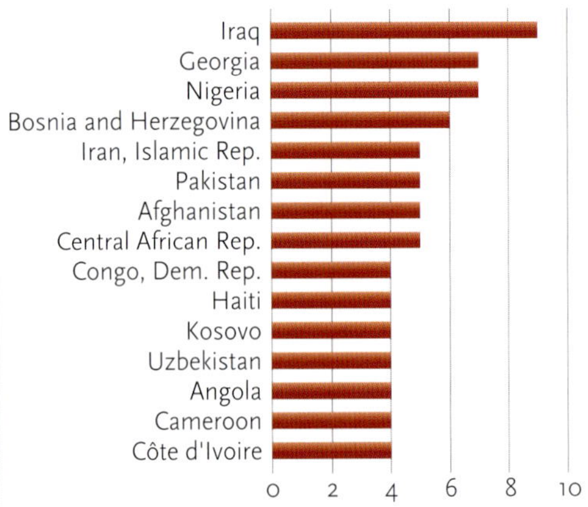

Source: MIGA-EIU Political Risk Survey 2010.

Political Risk Perceptions in CAF Economies

Although the link between political risk and FDI is far from straightforward, there is little dispute that risk perceptions influence foreign investment. A better understanding of investors' attitude toward political risk in CAF countries and how they manage it could, therefore, help illuminate their investment behavior. The reaction of investors to political perils in CAF countries, as manifested by the trends in FDI in these countries, is not uniform.

The literature on conflict has not focused much on foreign investors' reaction to, and mitigation of, political perils (see appendix 5 for a review of the literature). There are indications that various types of conflict affect FDI differently. In addition, most CAF countries, as noted earlier, suffer from structural weaknesses that are also likely to affect risk perceptions besides political violence.

FDI flows in Côte d'Ivoire during a 20-year period (figure 2.10) illustrate the typical impact of conflict on investment flows. Although the anticipated 1994 devaluation of the CFA franc had a severe negative impact on FDI, the decline was very short lived, and Côte d'Ivoire attracted sizable FDI inflows during most of the second half of the decade, when the country was still largely considered as a model of stability. The eruption of political conflict toward the end of the 1990s, however, resulted in a decline in FDI flows. Yet, FDI flows remained positive, most likely because violence was largely contained to a limited part of the country. Foreign investment continued to mirror Côte d'Ivoire's political situation, with an upswing following the creation of a government of national unity in 2002.

Figure 2.10 FDI flows in Côte d'Ivoire

$ million

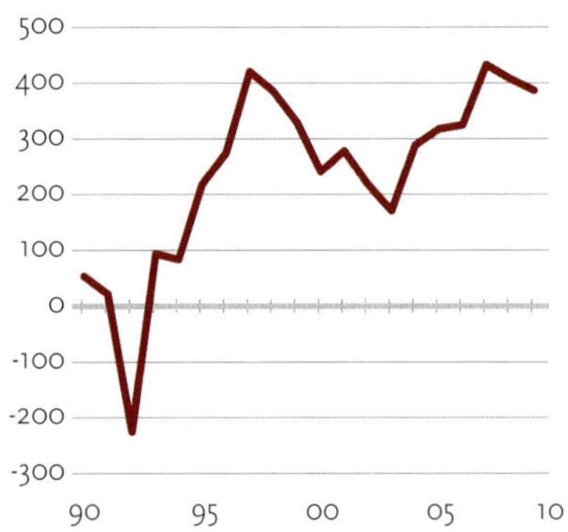

Source: World Bank estimates.

To better understand the impact of conflict and fragility on the perception and management of political risk, MIGA gauged the responses of investors involved in CAF countries (the MIGA-EIU CAF Investors Survey, see appendix 6). Those findings complement the findings of the MIGA-EIU Political Risk Survey 2010 (chapter 1 and appendix 2).

When compared to other investment challenges, political risk appears to be a far more salient issue for investors in CAF countries than for those operating in developing markets in general. A third of respondents considered it as the main obstacle to investing in CAF destinations (figure 2.11). Obstacles indirectly related to conflict and fragility—such as limited market size and, to a lesser extent, weak government institutions—also rank somewhat higher for investors in CAF countries than for those involved in developing countries overall. Given the importance of these other obstacles to foreign investment in CAF countries, the statistical analysis conducted by MIGA (explained next) attempted to control for variables related to market size and level of economic development in order to assess as closely as possible the political-risk impact on investments to CAF. This could less easily be isolated in the surveys, though. Conversely, fewer investors are concerned about economic and business considerations such as lack of qualified staff or macroeconomic instability in CAF countries relative to other developing countries.

Figure 2.11 Constraints for FDI in CAF states and developing countries

Percent of respondents

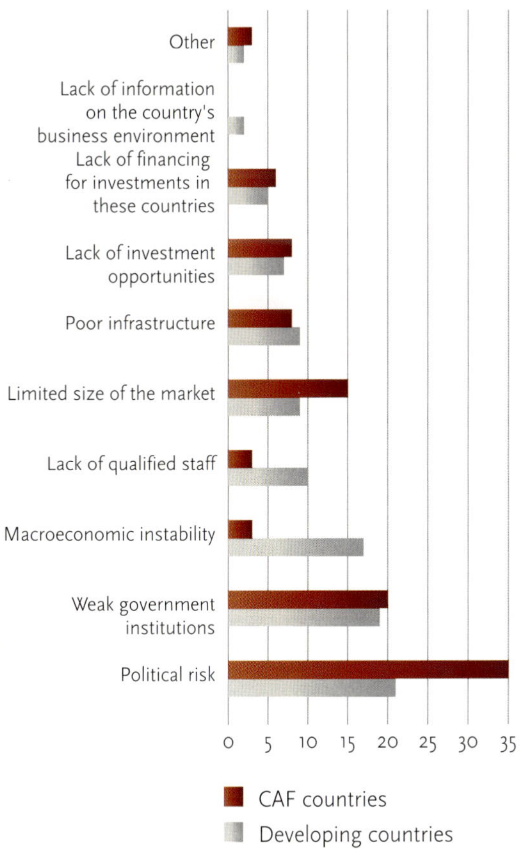

Source: MIGA-EIU Political Risk Survey 2010.

South-based MNEs with investments in CAF countries find political risk more challenging than other investment obstacles compared to their North-based counterparts. Similarly, a higher proportion of small firms than large ones rank political perils as a top challenge—although they cite access to financing as the main obstacle they face.

Both investors involved in CAF countries and those investing in developing countries are more worried about adverse government interventions—including regulatory changes, non-honoring of sovereign guarantees, currency restrictions, expropriation, and breach of contract—than about political violence (figure 2.12). Over 60 percent of investors in countries affected by conflict or considered fragile rank adverse regulatory changes as a main concern, a higher proportion than for those involved in developing countries. This ranking is likely to reflect the fact that these are the key concerns to investors in the extractive industries. In this sense, a driver for the differential in responses from the CAF and non-CAF countries appears to be the industry mix in each of these countries, which itself is driven by the sector characteristics (as detailed next).

War and terrorism, conversely, rank low relative to other risks for both sets of investors. This rank may reflect that in CAF countries, the main asset–given the importance of the primary sector—is the mineral underground, which is not prone to losses caused by violence. However, in other developing countries, the same result for a different sector mix must represent an inherent loss of a lower risk arising from war and civil disturbance. Although the risk of terrorism is by no means absent in developing countries, it appears to be perceived as primarily related to industrialized countries.[28]

Investors in CAF countries, moreover, rank concerns over civil disturbance (as opposed to war and to terrorism) significantly higher than those in developing countries in general, reflecting a more acute risk of conflict in these investment destinations. Yet, breach of contract—the main worry for investors in developing countries—is considered a major investment obstacle by less than one in five investors in CAF countries. This finding is somewhat surprising because extractive industries and infrastructure, both of which usually rely on contractual agreements with local governments, are often major areas of investment in CAF economies.

Figure 2.12 Political risks of most concern to foreign investors

Percent of respondents

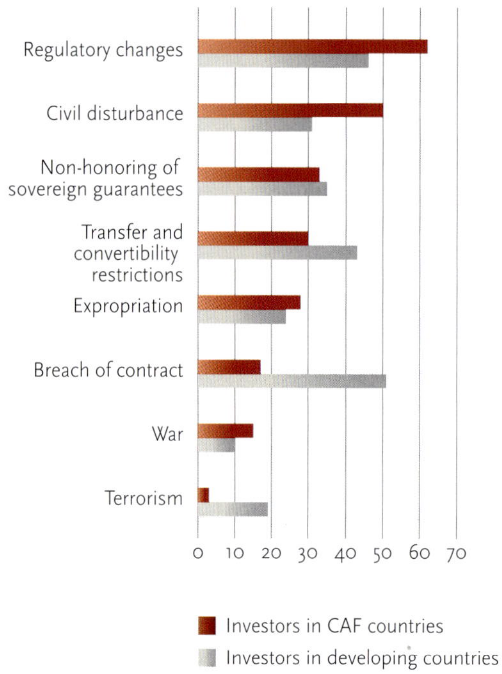

Source: MIGA-EIU Political Risk Survey 2010 and MIGA-EIU CAF Investors Survey.
Note: Percentages add up to more than 100 because of multiple selections.

A quarter of investors involved in CAF countries report having suffered losses resulting from political risks, primarily caused by civil disturbance and adverse regulatory changes. The highest proportion of investors having experienced losses in developing countries, however, suffered from government intervention—whether regulatory changes, breach of contract, transfer and convertibility restrictions, or non-honoring of sovereign guarantees (chapter 1).

Although losses associated with war or civil disturbance appear more frequent in CAF countries, the financial impact is often limited to partial asset destruction or temporary business interruption, which does not necessarily result in the investment being written off. Other political perils such as expropriation, moreover, generally translate into a total loss. The average size of losses, therefore, tends to be smaller in CAF countries than in developing economies, as confirmed by claims data from political risk insurers (chapter 3). MIGA's experience, while limited, also points in the same direction: three out of the five claims it has paid were due to the war and civil disturbance; yet the single expropriation loss that MIGA has paid to date dwarfed the cumulative losses from these three war and civil disturbance claims.

For investors in CAF states, past losses appear directly related to divestment: 22 percent of MNEs surveyed say that political risk in CAF countries has resulted in scaling back, canceling or delaying their investments (figure 2.13). Civil disturbance and regulatory changes—which, as mentioned earlier, caused losses to a significant proportion of respondents—were the risks to which investors were most sensitive.

Figure 2.13 Proportion of companies that have scaled back, canceled, or delayed investments in CAF states because of political risk

Percent of respondents

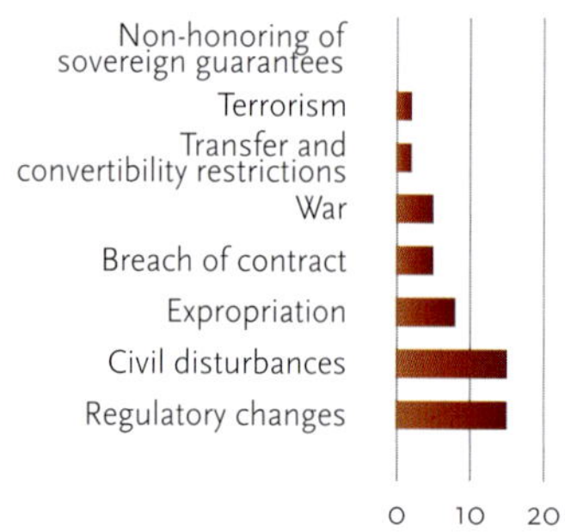

Source: MIGA-EIU CAF Investors Survey.

The survey results are consistent with findings from MIGA's review of over 45,000 greenfield investment projects, about 1,000 of which were located in CAF states. Two distinct analyses were carried out: one focused on the number of investment projects, and the other, on the investment amounts. As would be expected, the analysis confirmed the negative impact of conflict on investment[29]. The number of new investment projects was found to drop by 44 percent following civil war and by 34 percent when postconflict situations are included. The impact on greenfield investment by value was even more pronounced: conflict was found to result in a 90 percent decline (see appendix 7 for methodology and detailed results). This finding suggests that conflict affects larger investment projects more than smaller ones.

This statistical analysis does have limitations though. A significant part of the result remains unexplained by the conflict itself. As noted in an earlier section, violence is linked to a host of related challenges, from weakened institutions, to a breakdown in the rule of law and judicial systems, to drained public finances, and to increased corruption, all of which can discourage investment. Depleted public finances, for example, can increase the risk of non-honoring of sovereign guarantees, transfer restrictions, and expropriations. The breakdown of the rule of law contributes to regulatory uncertainty and undermines investors' ability to seek legal recourse. In a context of heightened global scrutiny, operating in a situation of conflict or political crisis can also threaten an investor's reputation (box 2.1). At the same time, political risk is pitted against other factors, such as the level and history of investors' involvement in a country (box 2.2). All these considerations, although only indirectly related to the conflict itself, nonetheless weigh on investment decisions.

Sector-Level Perspectives

Political risk perceptions and investment behavior in CAF countries appear to be determined to a large degree by sector characteristics. MIGA's investor surveys and statistical analysis largely suggest that both attitude to risk and the impact of conflict on investment decisions are heavily influenced by sectors of operation, resulting in FDI profiles in CAF economies that are significantly different from the rest of developing countries.

The following analysis, however, provides only partial and sometimes contradictory answers. In addition, some findings are ambiguous when it comes to sectors critical for these economies, such as extractive industries and telecommunications. More research is needed to fully explain the interaction between sector characteristics, political risk, and investment decisions in a context of fragility and conflict.

To decipher the behavior of investors in various sectors, three main channels of transmission of political risk to foreign investors in CAF countries have been identified as an initial framework of analysis:

- the possible destruction of assets resulting from conflict itself;
- the unavailability of inputs and adequate human resources resulting from the lack of infrastructure and from weak institutional and regulatory frameworks, all of which often characterize CAF economies; and
- abrupt declines in domestic demand, leading to lasting impoverishment that persists beyond the end of hostilities.

According to the above framework, most services—in particular financial services—would be unlikely to be the main source of investment in CAF countries, unlike in developing countries in general, where services account for most FDI. The main challenge would not be the risk of asset destruction—because services tend to rely more on intangible than tangible assets—but the demand shock resulting from conflict (box 2.2). Moreover, the extractive industry, with little links to the domestic economy and oriented toward exports, is not affected by demand shocks. Extractive investments are in theory particularly vulnerable to asset destruction resulting from their capital intensity. Yet, the concentration of those assets in one or two locations, sometimes offshore, makes them easier to secure, which partly mitigates the risk of destruction.

Actual investment flows confirm this analysis only in part, however. Although reliable FDI data by sector are not available for CAF countries, greenfield investments suggest that the primary sector—mostly extractive industries—has been receiving the lion's share of FDI in aggregate terms (figure 2.14). As noted earlier in this chapter, a significant proportion of countries prone to conflict or fragile are also dependent on natural resources, and the link between minerals and violence has been the subject of much debate and scrutiny (box 2.3).

Box 2.1 AngloGold Ashanti in the Democratic Republic of Congo

On June 1, 2005, AngloGold Ashanti faced an unexpected storm: a Human Rights Watch (HRW) report accused the mining company of providing financial and logistical assistance to an armed militia responsible for atrocities in the northeastern region of the Democratic Republic of Congo. The accusations, which received broad media coverage, came as a surprise and threatened the company's reputation and operations in the country.

AngloGold Ashanti was the first major foreign investor to return to the troubled northeastern region of the war-ravaged Democratic Republic of Congo. In 1996, Ashanti Goldfields purchased a stake in a joint venture that held an exploration and mining lease near Mongbwalu in the Ituri region, which sits on one of the richest gold fields in Africa. War halted operations in 1997, however, and the site was handed over to the local parastatal minority partner. Following the December 2002 peace agreement, Ashanti Goldfields—then in the process of merging with AngloGold—consulted its local joint venture partner, the interim government of the Democratic Republic of Congo, and the United Nations peacekeeping mission to explore whether a presence could be reestablished in the area and mining exploration conducted.

In light of the recent conflict, the persisting instability in the eastern part of the country, and the continued presence of militia elements, security remained an issue. The company, however, assessed the situation as sufficiently stable to reengage. In addition, a United Nations peacekeeping camp was to be established in the vicinity of the concession. As a result, AngloGold Ashanti set up an exploration camp in 2004, and unarmed security guards were recruited. Exploration drilling started in January 2005. The company, nonetheless, prepared emergency response and evacuation plans in case the conflict escalated again. As the project was in its early stages, financial investment was to be very gradual, thus limiting potential losses.

Besides keeping an active dialogue with the government and the United Nations, as well as constantly monitoring the situation, AngloGold Ashanti's risk-mitigation strategy also relied on relations with the local community. The long history of mining in the area predating AngloGold Ashanti's involvement had resulted in suspicions and grievances that needed to be addressed. The company, aware it needed to secure a "social license" to mine, supplied the neighboring public hospital with equipment and medication, and it repaired its water supply system, which had been down for seven years. Equipment and supplies have also been provided to local schools, and infrastructure such as roads, drainage, and power supply have been repaired and maintained.

The HRW report documented the intense competition among armed militia over access to gold in the Ituri region—where the central government had very little control—and the resulting atrocities committed against the local population. It accused AngloGold Ashanti of developing relations with one of the militias, the Nationalist and Integrationist Front (FNI), in exchange for security assurance and access to the concession. The nongovernmental organization (NGO) further stated that the company provided financial and logistical support to the group, indirectly furthering conflict and human rights abuses. It also argued that, although investment was desperately needed in the Democratic Republic of Congo, the company should have waited until it could work in the area without having to interact with warlords.

AngloGold Ashanti denied it had nurtured a relationship with the militia. Although admitting that some encounters with the FNI were unavoidable, it argued that cash and transport had been provided under duress and threats from the militia. There was also confusion surrounding freight landing taxes at the local airstrip, which the company initially thought legitimate and collected by the transitional government. The company stated that caving in to extortion was not part of its policy.

The fallout from the HRW report threatened AngloGold Ashanti's reputation and its relation with the government of the Democratic Republic of Congo and the local population; it could also undermine its efforts to obtain mining concessions in other countries. Relations with the government were ironed out, and the investor ramped up its interactions with NGOs, including HRW. Lessons were also learned about when and how to develop closer relations with local communities, and about gaining a better understanding of the situation on the ground. A forum of local leaders has been created to keep dialogue open, and AngloGold Ashanti is working with artisanal miners active in the area to introduce basic safety and environmental precautions. The company committed to continually review its operation and to withdraw from the area if the security situation deteriorated, or if its operation failed to enhance economic prospects—and the peace process—in the country.

The project has faced other hurdles. The legal and contractual environment in the Democratic Republic of Congo has been in flux after it launched a review and renegotiation of mining contracts in 2007. With a revised agreement with the Congolese authorities now in place and improved security in the area, the project is back on track. A feasibility study is planned for next year, with potential production starting a few years later.

NGO scrutiny has become an integral part of the business environment, however. In January 2010, CAFOD, a United Kingdom–based aid agency, published a report questioning the benefits of the mining project for the local population, and called for more transparency.

Source: MIGA, based on information provided by AngloGold Ashanti, Human Rights Watch, CAFOD, and secondary sources.

Box 2.2 The Weight of History: Old Mutual in Zimbabwe

Old Mutual, a global financial services provider, has deep African roots. Established in South Africa in 1845 as the Mutual Life Assurance Society of the Cape of Good Hope, it opened its first office in what is today known as Zimbabwe in 1927. Over time, Old Mutual expanded its business in the country from life insurance to mortgage finance, short-term insurance, pension funds, fund management, and real estate development. By the late 1990s, the company was a pillar of Zimbabwe's financial services industry, employing about 2,200 people who serve hundreds of thousands of clients.

Starting in the late 1990s, however, Zimbabwe sunk into political crisis and economic meltdown. In less than a decade, unemployment skyrocketed, while domestic demand collapsed. Hyperinflation destroyed asset values and wiped out savings. The local currency became worthless. A parallel economy developed, bypassing the formal financial system. Old Mutual's client base and assets melted away. Unable to invest offshore, the company converted cash into real assets as much as possible, investing in sectors such as mining or tourism, which were largely shielded from the collapse of local demand. To survive the collapse of local demand, it had to slim down and transform itself into a back office for the group's South African operations. At the worst of the crisis, Old Mutual's Zimbabwe business was written down to UK£2.

Old Mutual also got caught in the political crossfire. The group's shares listed on the Harare stock exchange—which once accounted for a fifth of the local market capitalization—were being used by the public and the business community as virtual currency. Comparing Old Mutual's share prices in Harare, Johannesburg, and London provided the basis for calculating a virtual exchange rate. In addition, share trading across the group's multiple listings was used to bypass currency transfer regulations. Local authorities threatened to delist the company and accused Old Mutual—which had moved its head office to the United Kingdom and was listed in London in 1999—of nurturing a political agenda and pushing for a change of regime. The company was threatened with expropriation.

At the same time, opposition supporters accused Old Mutual of shoring up the regime. By law, the company was required to hold government debt. In addition, part of its long-standing assets included shares in a media group considered as a ruling party mouthpiece.

Faced with the collapse of its local business, the intensifying political pressure from both sides, and the threats to its reputation, Old Mutual briefly considered closing up shop in Zimbabwe. Yet, clients and employees depended on the company, and Old Mutual's long history in the country weighed in favor of weathering the storm. By then, financial risks were minimal because the investment had already been written off, and the Zimbabwe business—although barely surviving—was self-sufficient.

The creation of a power-sharing government in 2008 has somewhat eased the political conflict, however, and reforms have fostered a modest economic recovery. The local currency has been abandoned, and hyperinflation reined in. Risks have not disappeared though: the political situation remains fragile; most international assistance is being held back; and the economic outlook is, therefore, still precarious. In addition, there is much debate and uncertainty over the authorities' plans to indigenize the economy, which could have a significant impact on foreign investors.

Figure 2.14 Greenfield cross-border investment flows to CAF countries by sector

Percent

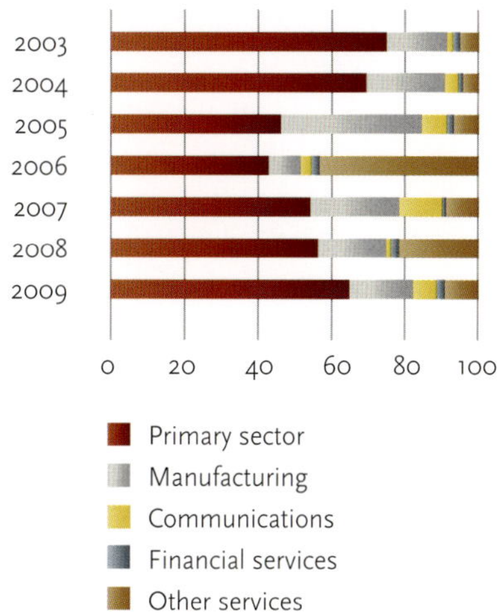

Source: fDi Markets database.

Yet, the service sector (communications, financial services, and other services) comes second after extractive industries, exceeding manufacturing in some years.[30] As the channels of transmission framework would suggest, the share of investment in financial services has indeed been minuscule. In most years, infrastructure, which is capital intensive and vulnerable to asset destruction, accounts for the bulk of investments in services. Telecommunications projects, which account for two-thirds of total investment commitments in infrastructure, remain attractive even in the presence of conflict because of the high value placed on accessing news and information in an uncertain environment, the weakness of fixed-line networks, and the low cellular penetration—which offer attractive growth potential.[31]

To better understand foreign investors' reaction to conflict, MIGA conducted statistical work analyzing greenfield investments in various sectors in conflict and nonconflict countries over the past decade. The cross-country analysis for each industry yielded the results depicted in figure 2.15 (where the negative coefficient indicates an unwillingness to invest in a conflict country compared to a nonconflict country and where the positive coefficient indicates that investors are more prone to invest in a conflict country than in a nonconflict country).

The sector-specific analysis confirms the conclusion of the country-level analysis: conflict results in an overall fall in investments. Although the two regression models yielded results that were not always consistent, different behaviors can be observed across sectors. First, the risk of asset destruction appears to weigh heavily on investment decisions: investments in industries with high fixed-capital intensity—such as real estate, automobiles and components, and technology hardware—appear highly deterred by conflict. Conversely, service industries (financial services or software and information technology [IT] services), with lower intensity of fixed capital, are less affected. The risk of asset destruction provides only part of the answer, however, because conflict appears to deter investments in commercial services much more than in energy.

Second, the risk of reduced domestic demand caused by conflict appears determinant as well. Investments in tradable industries show, ceteris paribus, a lower fall than in nontradable industries. For example, commercial services and hotels, restaurants, and leisure, which provide nontradable services, experience a

Old Mutual has established a constructive relationship with the transitional authorities, and accusations from both sides of the political divide have died down. Market research conducted locally confirmed that the company's reputation remains positive and its name is trusted. The uptake on recently launched financial products has been promising. Thanks to improved economic conditions, Old Mutual's Zimbabwean operation is once again profitable. Having successfully navigated a political and economic minefield, the company remains committed to Zimbabwe.

Source: MIGA, based on information provided by Old Mutual and secondary sources.

Box 2.3 FDI in Natural Resources and Political Violence

A number of resource-rich countries in the developing world have suffered recurrent conflicts, civil wars, and other forms of political violence. Oil-rich countries, for example, have a higher probability of facing conflict, while countries rich in minerals (gemstones) are more likely to suffer lengthier periods of conflict.[a] Resource-rich countries are often more likely to relapse into conflict than are resource-poor ones.[b]

Dependence on natural resources has been found in some studies to be closely correlated with the onset of conflict, either through attempts to control these resources or through grievances stemming from inequitable wealth sharing, which often coincides with weak state institutions or the presence of the "Dutch disease."[c] Revenues from the sale of natural resources may also be used to finance conflict or to undermine the return to peace, hence prolonging the duration of conflict. Multinational enterprises in the extractive sectors have themselves at times been implicated in the genesis or prolongation of conflict.[d] For example, international mining companies may trade in minerals sourced from mines that are used to finance lengthy civil wars.

Yet, FDI in natural resources can potentially promote political stability in CAF states by providing the capital and technical knowhow to exploit them, as well as to generate substantial fiscal revenues and to catalyze private investment. In light of both the magnitude of the investment and the time required for natural resource extraction, foreign investors adopt a longer-term horizon. In addition, investors in natural resources, bound by the geography of mineral deposits, have fewer choices when it comes to investment destinations than do those operating in other industries, and most assets cannot be relocated. As a result, they are often among the last ones to retreat in times of conflict and are among the first to return once violence subsides (see also box 2.2).

a Michael L. Ross, 2004, "What Do We Know about Natural Resources and Civil War?" *Journal of Peace Research*, 41: 337–56.

b Resource conflicts experience shorter postconflict peace durations than non-resource conflicts. See Helga Malmin Binningsbø and Siri Rustad, 2007, "Resource Conflicts, Resource Management and Postconflict Peace," paper presented at the annual meeting of the International Studies Association 48th Annual Convention, Chicago, IL.

c Paul Collier and Anke Hoeffler, 2004, "Greed and Grievance in Civil War," *Oxford Economic Papers*, 56: 563–95; Paul Collier, Anke Hoeffler and D. Rohner, 2009, "Beyond Greed and Grievance: Feasibility and Civil War," *Oxford Economic Papers*, 61: 1-27; Michael L. Ross, 2006, "A Closer Look at Diamonds, Oil and Civil War," *Annual Review of Political Science*, 9: 265–300. Other studies have not found a link between conflict and natural resource abundance (e.g., Christa Brunnschweiler and Erwin Bulte, 2008, "Natural Resources and Violent Conflict: Resource Abundance, Dependence and the Onset of Civil War," working paper 08/78, Center of Economic Research, ETH Zurich).

d John Bray, 2010, "Foreign Direct investment in Conflict-Affected Contexts," *International Alert*, Working Group for Development and Peace, Practice Note 3. In this context, the recently passed Wall Street Reform and Consumer Protection Act of 2010 in the United States places new reporting requirements on publicly traded companies that manufacture products using minerals deemed as financing conflict in the Democratic Republic of Congo and neighboring countries.

steep fall in greenfield investments, while energy or consumer staples, which produce tradable goods, do not exhibit any significant decrease in investments.

Figure 2.15 Investments by sector in conflict countries

Conflict dummy: regression coefficients

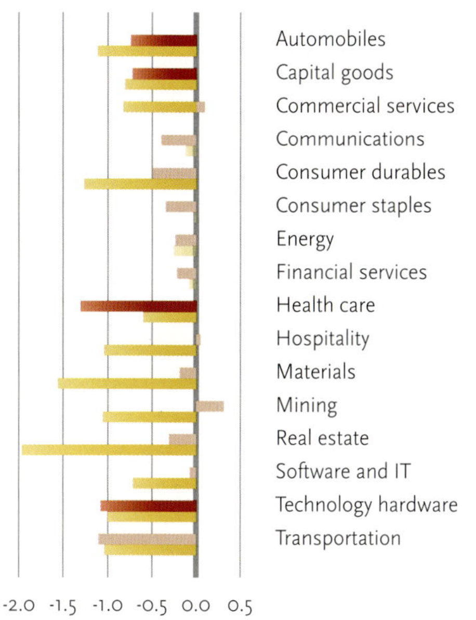

Source: MIGA internal analysis and appendix 7.
Note: Solid bars represent statistical significance at 10 percent or less. IT=information technology.

Third, relying on a local supply chain and high-skilled personnel makes companies vulnerable to the increase in input costs caused by conflict. As a result, high-technology industries (e.g., technology hardware, software and IT services, and capital goods) tend to be more deterred than lower-technology industries such as consumer staples or consumer durables. However, extractive industries, with relatively shielded inputs, do not face this risk. The statistical analysis indeed suggests that investments in the energy sector do not react much to conflict (although metals and mining do, by a factor of around 60 percent).

In addition, investor surveys provide insights into risk perceptions across sectors. Across most sectors, a higher proportion of respondents operating in CAF countries consider political risk as their main investment constraint relative to other challenges, compared to those in developing countries (figure 2.16). Investors in manufacturing—usually heavily relying on fixed assets—and in services appear more concerned about political perils in CAF economies not only compared to other sectors, but also relative to respondents operating in developing countries in general. This concern is consistent with the idea of risk transmitted primarily through asset destruction, supply chains, and demand shocks.

The lowest proportion of investors that rank political risk in CAF countries as their main challenge is in the primary sector. In addition, there is not much difference between their perception in CAF and developing countries in general. This finding is most likely a reflection that, compared to other sectors, a higher proportion of extractive industry investments in developing countries are located in fragile and conflict-prone destinations. It could also be due to the long-term horizons of these investments. Because the choice of investment destinations and the possibilities of relocation are much narrower than in other sectors, the focus is on when, rather than whether, to engage in a CAF country and how to mitigate political risk, as illustrated in the case study of AngloGold Ashanti in the Democratic Republic of Congo (see box 2.1).

Figure 2.16 Proportion of firms that consider political risk to be the most significant constraint for FDI

Percent of respondents

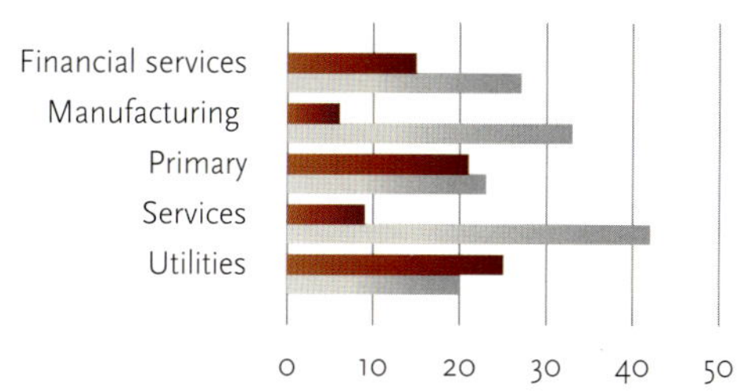

Source: MIGA-EIU Political Risk Survey 2010 and MIGA-EIU CAF Investors Survey.

If one looks across sectors, risk perceptions sometimes seem to be at odds with the behavior of greenfield investments identified in the quantitative analysis cited earlier. For instance, respondents in financial services—one of the sectors least likely to react to conflict according to figure 2.15—appear to be among the most sensitive to political risk in CAF economies (figure 2.16) compared to other industries. The financial services industry has been identified in the analytical framework on the basis of the three transmission channels (see earlier) as an industry likely to be heavily influenced by the collapse of domestic demand resulting from conflict. However, the statistical analysis and survey results appear broadly in line when it comes to telecommunications, a sector whose risk perceptions appear relatively low. Similarly, the manufacturing sector's high aversion to risk compared to most other sectors appears to confirm the statistical analysis based on actual investments.

One potential explanation for the gap between risk perception and investment behavior is potential profit: the potential for high returns over a short payback period is likely to convince some investors to operate in a high-risk environment. Indeed, when asked to provide the main reasons why political risk is not a deterrent in CAF economies, two main reasons that survey respondents cited—regardless of their sector, company size, or geographical origin—were that (i) business opportunities outweighed risks, or (ii) potential losses were limited (figure 2.17).

Figure 2.17 Why is political risk not a deterrent to investments in CAF countries?

Percent of responses

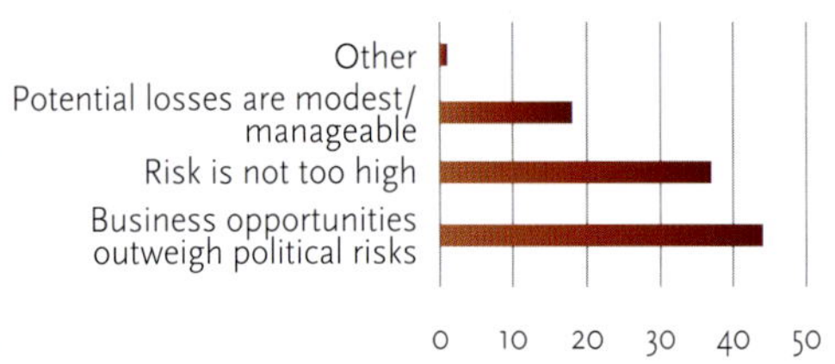

Source: MIGA-EIU Political Risk Survey 2010 and MIGA-EIU CAF Investors Survey.

MNEs that feel they are able to effectively protect their investments even in environments they perceive as high risk—and therefore limit their losses—are more likely to invest. This observation suggests that risk mitigation is a key determinant of investment in CAF countries.

Corporate Approaches to Political Risk Management in CAF Economies

Ninety percent of the firms that currently invest in CAF countries actively manage their exposures to political risk. Like investors in developing countries, MIGA-EIU CAF Investors Survey respondents overwhelmingly favor non-contractual tools to mitigate political risks (figure 2.18) and typically use a variety of mechanisms to do so (box 2.4).

Figure 2.18 Tools used by investors to mitigate political risk

Percent of respondents

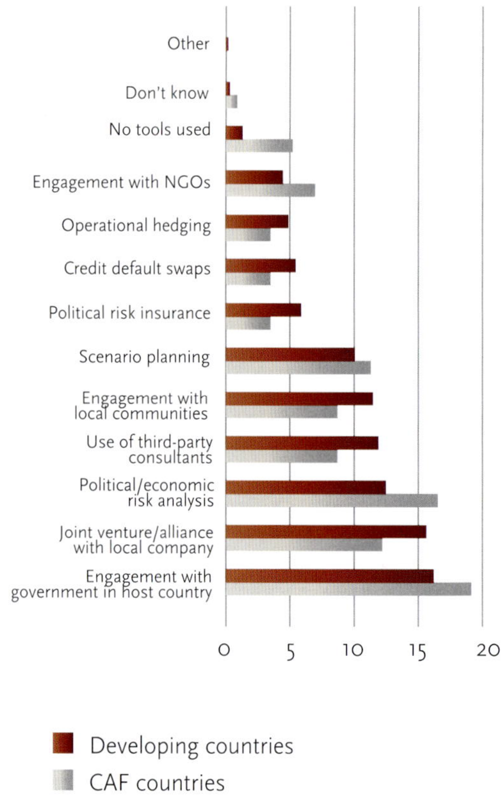

Source: MIGA-EIU Political Risk Survey 2010 and MIGA-EIU CAF Investors Survey.

Box 2.4 Mitigating Risk on Several Fronts: SN Power in Nepal

SN Power, an international, Norwegian-based hydropower company, illustrates the many ways that foreign investors mitigate political risks in developing countries. In the early 1990s, SN Power's parent company, Statkraft, decided to expand overseas following 100 years of hydropower experience in Norway, where expansion opportunities had become limited. Nepal offered attractive business opportunities.

The $140 million power project in Khimti—about 100 km east of Kathmandu—was the first private sector power project in Nepal. Political change and the establishment of a multiparty parliament in 1991, together with new business legislation, made the country increasingly attractive to foreign investors. The project structure for Khimti was carefully designed to address a number of technical, regulatory, and commercial risks. The involvement of multilateral lenders and export credit agencies offered additional comfort and risk mitigation.

At the time, the risk of widespread political violence appeared remote. Although few insurers were ready to underwrite investments in Nepal at the time, the investor managed to contract political risk insurance (PRI) from MIGA to protect the equity investment against the risks of restrictions on currency convertibility and transfer, expropriation, and war and civil disturbance.

The power plant was commissioned in 2000. Although an insurgency had developed in the mid-1990s, few incidents were reported in the Khimti area until 2001. When the political and security situation deteriorated, the army was deployed in the region. In October 2002, insurgents sabotaged the intake of the Khimti facility, as well as a small hydropower plant providing rural electrification to neighboring villages. Yet, the damage was small compared to the scale of the investment, and support from the local community prevented escalation and further incidents. Compensation was received through the investor's PRI, and the power plant continued operating.

Over the years, SN Power has continued to develop social programs in Nepal. In partnership with development agencies, the company has provided local electrification, has facilitated the provision of irrigation and drinking water, has established and supports an elementary school, and now operates a clinic—all of which benefit the population living around the power plant and enhance local support for the project. The involvement of a Nepalese shareholder has been important to better understand local dynamics and to develop a constructive relationship with both the local community and the government. In addition, the Norwegian Development Agency and the Norwegian Embassy in Kathmandu have provided valuable country expertise, besides financial and technical assistance.

Although the insurgency officially came to an end in 2006, political risks have not disappeared. In light of Nepal's political situation, the future regulatory framework and protection for long-term investors appear uncertain. The uncertain political landscape has also resulted in delays for investors waiting for licenses or permits. In addition, the peace agreement has not fully put an end to violence, and safety remains a concern.

After years operating in Nepal, however, SN Power is confident it can assess and manage political perils. The company—keen to respond to local power needs and to tap into the power-export potential to India—is now contemplating other investments in the country.

Source: MIGA, based on information provided by SN Power and secondary sources.

Yet, there are significant differences between investors operating in CAF economies and those involved in other developing countries. The proportion of investors in CAF countries that report they do not mitigate risks at all is significantly higher than in other developing countries. At the same time, the uncertain and volatile environment in many CAF investment destinations could explain why a higher proportion of respondents operating in these countries assess and monitor risks through risk analysis and scenario planning. Similarly, a significantly higher share than those in developing countries engages with local governments, suggesting that investors in more stable host countries may have greater confidence in existing institutions and legal frameworks, thus reducing the need for close interaction with government authorities.

Each sector's specific vulnerability and attitude to risk, as outlined earlier, are also likely to determine the relevance of PRI as a mitigation tool. Investors in CAF countries appear to rely less on PRI than MNEs operating in developing countries in general (figure 2.18). This gap could be due to a mismatch between investors' specific concerns and mitigation needs in fragile countries on the one hand, and to what the PRI industry offers in these destinations on the other hand.

The next chapter examines attitudes of investors operating in CAF countries toward PRI in more detail, as well as industry trends in developing countries and in fragile or conflict-affected investment destinations. PRI may play a role as one of many risk-mitigating strategies deployed by investors, as illustrated in the Nepal case (box 2.4). Understanding the conditions in which, at the margin, the availability of PRI tips the balance of the investment decision in favor of going forward remains an area of future research.

Chapter Two—Endnotes

1 The list of resource-dependent (or resource-rich) countries comprises those whose primary sector accounts for more than 20 percent of GDP. These countries also underwent a qualitative review to assess whether they could be classified as resource dependent from the point of view of the impact of the primary sector on political and economic decision making.

2 The CPIA index is a composite measure of economic management, structural and social policies, and the quality of public-sector institutions. The selection of fragile countries and territories by the World Bank is based on a rating of 3.2 or below (out of a maximum of 5).

3 Ejaz Ghani and Lakshmi Iyer, 2010, "Conflict and Development: Lessons from South Asia," *Economic Premise*, No. 31, September. For a definition of civil wars, see Nicholas Sambanis, 2004, "What Is Civil War? Conceptual and Empirical Complexities of an Operational Definition," *Journal of Conflict Resolution*, 48: 814-58.

4 Collier and Hoeffler, 2004, "Greed and Grievance in Civil Wars," *Oxford Economic Papers*, 56: 563–95; James D. Fearon and David D. Laitin, 2003, "Ethnicity, Insurgency, and Civil War," *American Political Science Review*, 97: 75–90.

5 World Bank, Fragile and Conflict-Affected Countries, http://web.worldbank.org/WBSITE/EXTERNAL/PROJECTS/STRATEGIES/EXTLICUS/0,,menuPK:511784~pagePK:64171540~piPK:64171528~theSitePK:511778,00.html.

6 E. Miguel, S. Satyanath, and E. Sergenti, 2004, "Economic Shocks and Civil Conflict: An Instrumental Variables Approach," *Journal of Political Economy*, 112: 725–53; O. Dube and J. F. Vargas, 2009, "Commodity Price Shocks and Civil Conflict: Evidence from Colombia," Working Paper, Harvard University and UCLA.

7 Ejaz Ghani and Lakshmi Iyer, 2010.

8 Paul Collier and Anke Hoeffler, 2003, "Aid, Policy and Peace: Reducing the Risks of Civil Conflict," World Bank Conflict Prevention and Reconstruction Unit, Note No. 9. http://siteresources.worldbank.org/INTRANETSOCIALDEVELOPMENT/Resources/CPR9blue.pdf.

9 Paul Collier, 2007, "Post-Conflict Recovery: How Should Policies Be Distinctive?" Centre for Study of African Economies, Department of Economics, Oxford University, May. http://users.ox.ac.uk/~econpco/research/pdfs/PostConflict-Recovery.pdf.

10 Paul Collier, L. Elliott, H. Hegre, A. Hoeffler, M. Reynal-Querol, and N. Sambanis, 2003, "Breaking the Conflict Trap: Civil War and Development Policy," Washington, DC: World Bank.

11 OECD, 2010, "Ensuring Fragile States Are Not Left Behind: Summary Report 2010," Paris: OECD.

12 Dilip Ratha, Sanket Mohapatra, and Ani Silwal, 2010, "Outlook for Remittance Flows 2010-11: Remittance Flows to Developing Countries Remained Resilient in 2009, Expected to Recover During 2010–11," *Migration and Development Brief*, No.12.

13 The group of countries defined as fragile states used by the OECD is not identical to the list of countries used in the analysis for this report.

14 Excluding China and India.

15 OECD, 2010, *Annual Report: Resource Flows to Fragile and Conflict-Affected States 2010*, Paris: OECD.

16 World Bank estimates.

17 World Bank estimates.

18 United States Bureau of Economic Analysis, 2009, *Survey of Current Business*, September.

19 Ministry of Commerce, 2008, *Statistical Bulletin of China's Outward Foreign Direct Investment*, Beijing: Ministry of Commerce. Other important source countries (e.g., United Kingdom, France, and Japan) do not provide information at the level of detail needed to single out the CAF states.

20 World Bank, 2010, *Investing Across Borders*, Washington, DC: World Bank.

21 Out of a worldwide total of 2,755 treaties.

22 UNCTAD, International Investment Agreements database.

23 Croatia and Mozambique were no longer considered CAF economies in 2010.

24 UNCTAD, 2009, "How Post-Conflict Countries Can Attract and Benefit from FDI: Lessons from Croatia and Mozambique," Geneva: UNCTAD. http://www.unctad.org/templates/webflyer.asp?docid=13949&intItemID=2068&lang=1.

25 For a discussion of the outcomes of privatization in conflict and postconflict environments, see UNDP, 2008, *Post-Conflict Economic Recovery: Enabling Local Ingenuity*, New York: UNDP.

26 In Eritrea, for instance, the ratio of FDI to GDP has been over 36 percent since 1998.

27 World Bank estimates.

28 Swiss Re, 2010, "Terrorism Risk Still Looms Large." http://www.swissre.com/rethinking/Terrorism_risk_still_looms_large.html.

29 MIGA tested the control variables and found that they are statistically significant at the 1 percent level, which indicates robustness of the findings (see appendix 7, which also contains a brief outline of the methodology used).

30 See also John Bray, 2005, "International Companies and Post-Conflict Reconstruction: Cross-Sectoral Comparisons," World Bank Social Development Paper No. 22, February.

31 Agnieszka Konkel and Richard Heeks, 2009, "Challenging Conventional Views on Mobile Telecommunications Investment: Evidence from Conflict Zones," *Development in Practice*,19: 414–20. See also Knowledge@Wharton, 2009. "An Industry on the Line: Telecommunications in Afghanistan," March 26.

32 MIGA conducted a series of analysis of greenfield project-level data (described in appendix 7), and focused on two different regression models. First, MIGA conducted an industry (sector) panel analysis, where a panel for each sector and country-year was created. Second, a cross-sectional analysis was conducted, seeking to collapse the time dimension (compared to the panel analysis) and to analyze only yearly averages.

CHAPTER THREE

THE POLITICAL RISK INSURANCE INDUSTRY

Overview

The political risk insurance (PRI)[1] industry has weathered the global crisis well. Premium revenues reported by members of the Berne Union[2] (BU)—the leading association of investment insurers and export credit agencies (ECAs) (box 3.1)—increased in 2009, in spite of the 6 percent contraction in the investment insurance portfolio. Claims in investment insurance have remained modest, particularly when compared to losses suffered on the export credit segment, and capacity remains more than adequate to cover existing demand. The private PRI market has held steady. Unlike in the aftermath of previous crises, no reduction of capacity has been reported, and reinsurance remains available. Having declined in 2009, new business reported by BU members is picking up again in 2010, partly reflecting the expected recovery of foreign direct investment (FDI) flows (chapter 1). This increase is resulting in a recovery of the maximum limit of liability, and the industry expects these positive trends to accelerate over the next few years.

Box 3.1 The Berne Union

The Berne Union (BU) was founded in 1934 in order to promote international acceptance of sound principles in export credit and investment insurance and to exchange information relating to these activities. Today, the BU has 73 members (including Prague Club members) comprising mainly export credit agencies (ECAs), multilaterals, and private insurers (appendix 9). Most ECAs and multilaterals are BU members, as are large private insurers such as AIG (now Chartis Insurance), which joined in 1999, followed by Zurich and Sovereign Risk Insurance Ltd. In October 2008, Hiscox became the first private insurer underwriting in Lloyd's to join the BU. In 2009, ECAs accounted for about 66 percent of the BU's outstanding investment PRI portfolio, private members for 29 percent and multilaterals for 5 percent.

The BU's Prague Club (appendix 9) was started in 1993 with funding from the European Bank for Reconstruction and Development. It is an information exchange network for new and maturing insurers of export credit and investment. The Prague Club supports members' efforts to develop their export credit and investment insurance facilities by hosting technical discussions at twice-yearly meetings, as well as ad hoc information exchanges. A number of Prague Club members have gone on to meet the requirement for full BU membership.

The BU plays an important role in bringing together the public and private insurers to enhance cooperation and information sharing. Members meet on a regular basis to discuss industry trends and challenges. In recent years, there has been a concerted effort on the part of the BU Secretariat to promote transparency and disclosure in the industry and to represent member interests in order to promote global trade and investment.

Source: The Berne Union.

When it comes to conflict-affected and fragile (CAF) countries, however, the PRI industry remains generally cautious. Cover for most CAF countries is limited and restrictive, reflecting the industry's risk perceptions and, in some cases, foreign policy restrictions such as sanctions. Most of the PRI underwritten in these investment destinations is provided by a small number of insurers and is concentrated in a handful of resource-rich countries, mirroring the pattern of FDI flows (chapter 2). Although the proportion of claims relative to PRI portfolio in CAF countries has largely been in line with losses in other developing countries over the past few years, the profile of losses differs: CAF countries are responsible for most civil disturbance claims, but almost none are for expropriation.

Multilateral PRI providers, because of their mandate and ownership structures, can be in a better position than private insurers or export credit agencies (ECAs) to provide cover in investment destinations considered riskier, such as CAF countries. They are, therefore, well placed to play a catalyst role in expanding market capacity for these destinations not only by providing PRI directly, but also by mobilizing reinsurance and coinsurance for investments in destinations that may otherwise not have been considered, as highlighted through a number of initiatives already in place or in preparation.

After the Crisis: Recent Trends in the PRI Industry

The PRI industry (box 3.2) continues to be well positioned to respond to growth in demand for PRI as a modest recovery from the global downturn appears to be gaining traction. Demand for PRI slumped during the financial crisis in 2009 as funding for ongoing projects was put on hold or canceled, but it picked up again in the first half of 2010, reflecting the modest recovery in FDI (chapter 1).

Demand for PRI (box 3.3) is related to FDI flows, although the relation is neither linear (figure 3.1) nor well understood.[3] New demand for PRI slowed down in line with FDI flows to developing countries, which slumped by 40 percent in 2009 (chapter 1). The ratio between investment PRI and FDI remained stable at around 10 percent in 2009, consistent with levels observed over the past few years. This suggests that the global economic downturn and the evolution of political risk perceptions (chapter 1) have not resulted in heavier reliance on PRI. The relation between FDI and PRI is similar whether flows or stocks are considered. These results clearly indicate that PRI is one of many risk-mitigation tools that are used by foreign investors. How and why it interacts with other risk-mitigation tools (anywhere from local engagement strategies to global insurance policies along other lines that overlap with PRI) is a subject of future research. It is in the context of this interaction that the idea of whether or not there is a market failure in the PRI industry has to be considered.

Figure 3.1 Ratio of PRI to FDI for developing countries

Percent

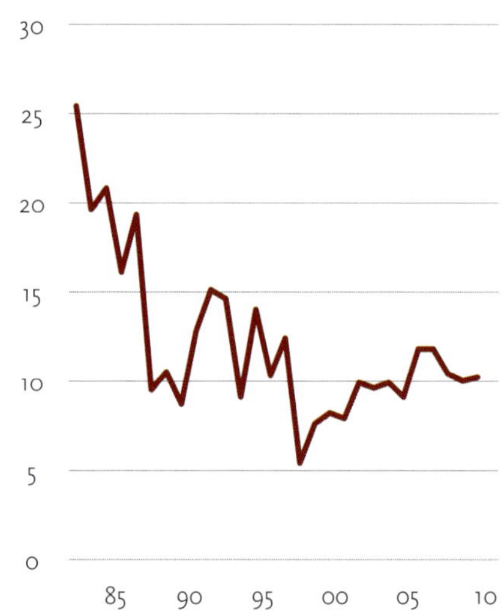

Source: BU and World Bank.
Note: Data for PRI are from BU members only.

Confirming last year's observations, the PRI market appears to have been stable throughout the financial crisis. Although many insurers have indicated that the volume of business written has declined as there has been a dearth of projects, other aspects of the market have changed little, and PRI providers remained willing, albeit more cautious, to underwrite projects.

Demand

Reflecting the decline in FDI flows, the amount of new business in investment PRI declined in 2009. Following several years of double-digit growth

Box 3.2 Overview of the PRI Industry

The political risk insurance (PRI) industry includes three broad categories of providers and covers both export or trade credit and investment insurance. For this report, PRI refers to investment insurance. The public PRI market comprises both national and multilateral PRI providers. The private market's PRI falls into two main categories: (i) political risk activities similar to that of the public insurers, such as coverage for investments in developing countries against expropriation, political violence, and other such risks; and (ii) developing country nonpayment insurance covering contract frustration and default by governments.

The National PRI Providers

The providers comprise national export credit agencies (ECAs) and investment insurance entities. They focus on cross-border trade and investment, generally for constituents in their own countries.

The Multilaterals

Multilaterals include the African Trade Insurance Agency (ATI), the Asian Development Bank, the Inter-American Development Bank, the Arab Investment and Export Credit Guarantee Corporation (Dhaman), the Islamic Corporation for the Insurance of Investment and Export Credit (ICIEC), and the Multilateral Investment Guarantee Agency (MIGA). The World Bank, the Asian Development Bank, and the Inter-American Development Bank also provide risk-mitigation instruments, such as partial risk guarantees.[a]

The Private PRI Market

The private market includes about 20 Lloyd's syndicates (appendix 8) and about eight private insurance companies. The majority of private insurers are based in three insurance centers—London, Bermuda, and the United States (primarily New York City)—and several of the larger insurers have offices in Singapore; Hong Kong SAR, China; Sydney; and elsewhere. As well as traditional equity PRI, the private market offers protection for a wide variety of developing-country payment risks, either for political perils alone or comprehensive nonpayment cover. Brokers play an important role in promoting and sourcing PRI for the private market. This market segment is dynamic: over the past year, some players have exited the PRI market, while new entrants have appeared.

The Reinsurers

Reinsurance companies write PRI-related coverage for both trade and investment. Reinsurance is an underlying factor driving both pricing and capacity in the private market. Some of the top reinsurers include Munich Re and Hannover Re of Germany, Swiss Re of Switzerland, and Berkshire Hathaway/General Re of the United States. ECAs and multilaterals also participate as reinsurers of PRI, although on a smaller scale.

Source: Data on national providers are from Berne Union, and data on private providers are from Gallagher London.

a A partial risk guarantee covers private lenders against the risk of government failure to honor contractual obligations relating to private projects.

Box 3.3 Political Risk Insurance and Its Benefits

Political Risk Insurance (PRI) captures most, but not all, noncommercial risks. It covers political events, including the direct and indirect actions of host governments that negatively impact investments and are not properly compensated for. This report focuses on investment insurance.

In addition to providing compensatory value in the event of claims, PRI can help investors access finance—often on better terms, thus increasing the tenors and size of available loans. Investors are often required to get this insurance in order to obtain financing from banks. For lenders, PRI can provide regulatory relief from country risk-provisioning requirements. When provided by multilateral and large national insurers, PRI can also help deter harmful actions by host governments, can help resolve investment disputes, and can provide access to best practices in environmental and social standards.

Motivations driving the public and private segments of the market are fundamentally different, which is partly reflected in the cover they are able to provide. National insurers have strict mandates from their authorities to serve constituent interests and are bound by foreign policy considerations. Multilateral providers ensure that their activities are consistent with broad developmental goals. Private providers, however, are motivated by the need to make profit. As a result, public and multilateral providers are usually able to offer longer tenors and higher capacity than can private insurers, but private providers can be more responsive to customer needs for product variations or complementary products.

The following are the political risks commonly insured by the PRI industry. There are differences in the terminology and definitions used by the various insurers, particularly between the public and private insurers.

Expropriation
PRI protects against losses caused by host government actions that may reduce or eliminate ownership or control. It covers outright confiscations, expropriations, and nationalizations, as well as losses resulting from a series of acts that over time have an expropriatory effect.

Currency Inconvertibility and Transfer Restrictions
PRI protects against losses arising from an investor's inability to convert local currency into foreign exchange and to transfer it out of the host country. It also covers excessive delays in acquiring foreign exchange. Typically, this coverage applies to the interruption of interest payments or repatriation of capital or dividends resulting from currency restrictions. It does not cover devaluation risk.

Political Violence (War, Terrorism, and Civil Disturbance)
PRI protects against losses resulting from the damage of tangible assets or business interruption caused by war, insurrection, rebellion, revolution, civil war, vandalism, sabotage, civil disturbance, strikes, riots, and terrorism. Coverage usually applies to politically motivated acts. Certain insurers offer terrorism coverage on a stand-alone basis to supplement property insurance policies, which have largely excluded terrorism as a peril since September 11, 2001. Terrorism insurance increasingly offers cover against broader political violence risks.

(figure 3.2), members of the BU—the largest grouping of PRI providers—underwrote only $36 billion of new business in 2009, a decline of over 38 percent from 2008. Lloyd's new activity in that line has been estimated at another $40–50 billion.

New business recorded by BU members is picking up strongly, however, reflecting in part the modest recovery in FDI (chapter 1). It increased by over 80 percent in the first half of 2010 compared to the same period in 2009.

Sixty-five percent of the BU's new business in investment PRI in 2009 and 74 percent in the first half of 2010 was underwritten by public insurers. Their share in BU new business has been growing steadily from 50 percent in 2005, and the increase in 2009 and 2010 is the result of the underwriting of a few large projects. Over this period, the share of multilaterals has remained constant at about 3 percent, while private providers' share has declined.

The volume of liability held by BU investment insurers dropped to $137.1 billion in 2009, a decline of almost 6 percent compared to 2008. During this period, however, it also appears that fewer investors chose to terminate their insurance contracts early. Reflecting the recovery in new business, the maximum limit of liability totaled over $142 billion as of June 2010, an increase of 7.7 percent in 12 months and close to the 2007 level. About two-thirds of the portfolio was held by public PRI providers.

Figure 3.2 New PRI of BU members

$ billion

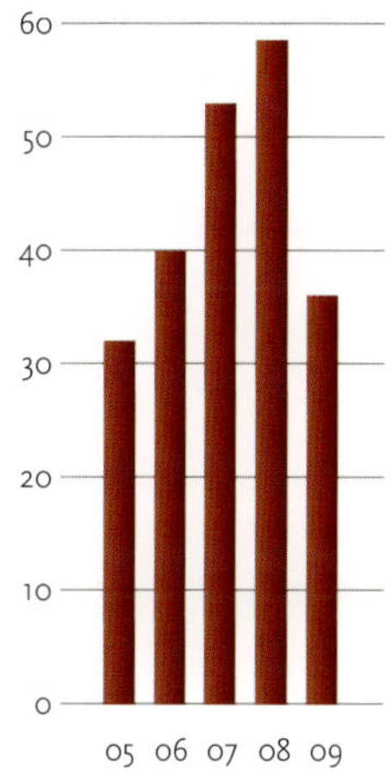

Source: Berne Union.
Note: Berne Union members only.

Breach of Contract/Arbitration Award Default
PRI protects against losses arising from a host government's breach or repudiation of a contractual agreement with an investor. Claims are usually payable only after an investor has invoked a dispute resolution mechanism (such as arbitration), has obtained an award for damages, and the host government has failed to honor the award.

Non-honoring of Sovereign Financial Obligations
PRI protects against losses resulting from a government's failure to make a payment when due under an unconditional financial payment obligation or guarantee given in favor of a project that otherwise meets an insurer's requirements. It does not require the investor to obtain an arbitral award. This coverage is usually applicable in situations when a sovereign's financial payment obligation is unconditional and not subject to defenses.

Source: MIGA and market consultations.

Some PRI providers, particularly private insurers that are based in key insurance markets such as London, reported an uptake in the number of inquiries for investment insurance, especially for expropriation and non-honoring coverage. These inquiries have come primarily from the power and extractive industries sectors. For the majority of underwriters, this uptake has not yet translated into new business. This finding can be partly due to the lead time required by projects in these sectors and the stage during the project cycle when the PRI provider becomes involved, as well as the time required to underwrite the projects. Conversely, a number of insurers, particularly ECAs, indicated that there had been little to no demand for PRI and that they had not underwritten any new projects during 2009 and into 2010. Surveyed PRI providers did not report any increase in policy cancelations, however.

Figure 3.3 New PRI business of North- and South-based investment insurance providers

$ billion

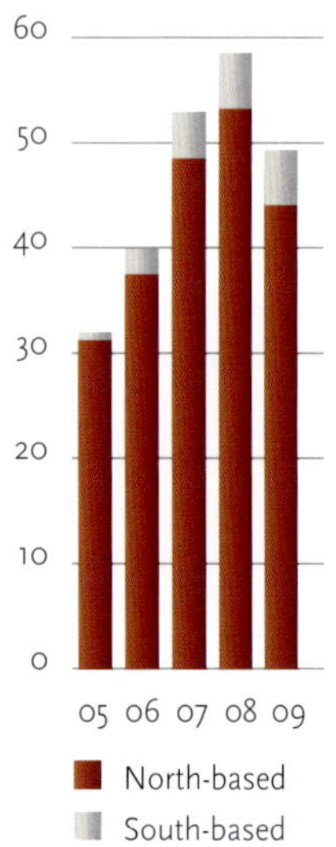

Source: Berne Union.
Note: Berne Union members only.

As the global financial and economic crisis continues to unwind, investment is expected to recover (chapter 1) and access to credit—although still tight—to slowly ease. As a result, the number of PRI inquiries translating into operational projects should increase, and most insurers contacted for this report expect the demand for investment PRI to pick up over the next 12 to 36 months.

The share of PRI provided by BU members from developing countries is expected to continue rising (figure 3.3), reflecting the emergence of South-based investors (chapter 1) and active policy from Sinosure, China's ECA, to promote outward FDI. In 2009, PRI providers from developing countries accounted for 11 percent of the BU's new business, up from 2.5 percent in 2005.

Capacity

According to both public and private insurers, there has been very little, if any, change to capacity available to underwrite investment PRI during the past 12 months. In addition, very few anticipate any change in capacity in the short term. Given the low levels of losses in the investment insurance segment compared to trade credit insurance, PRI underwriters did not face the same requirement to reduce cover to try to minimize losses. The longer-term, noncancelable nature of PRI contracts, compared to trade credit insurance, results in more stability, as providers have little flexibility to modify existing contracts in the event of an economic downturn or the rise of political instability.

Industry data for the private PRI market indicate that the capacity in this market segment increased from $1.2 billion to $1.3 billion per project in 2009.[4] In the first half of 2010, Lloyd's capacity remained constant. During that period, Chubb—a major private provider—exited the PRI business, while another company halved its capacity, resulting in a $125 million reduction in the company segment of the private market (figure 3.4). Chubb's exit reduced insurance supply for longer tenors (up to 10 years) in the private PRI market, where close to 60 percent of capacity is available for five years or less.[5] The lower demand for PRI and the emergence of new entrants, such as Ironshore and LUA, however, softened the impact of these changes. In July 2010, the private market was still able to underwrite $1.2 billion worth of PRI per project, similar to the level observed in July 2008. Unlike in the aftermath of the attacks of September 11, 2001—which led to a crisis in the general insurance market and a subsequent squeeze on PRI capacity—the general insurance market has weathered the global financial crisis relatively well, and current conditions have been relatively benign for the PRI segment. As a result, capacity in the private segment of political risk insurance has not declined significantly (as figure 3.4 illustrates, the Lloyd's market has remained stable, and the remaining private markets have fallen off slightly).

Figure 3.4 Available private market capacity, total possible maximum per risk

$ million

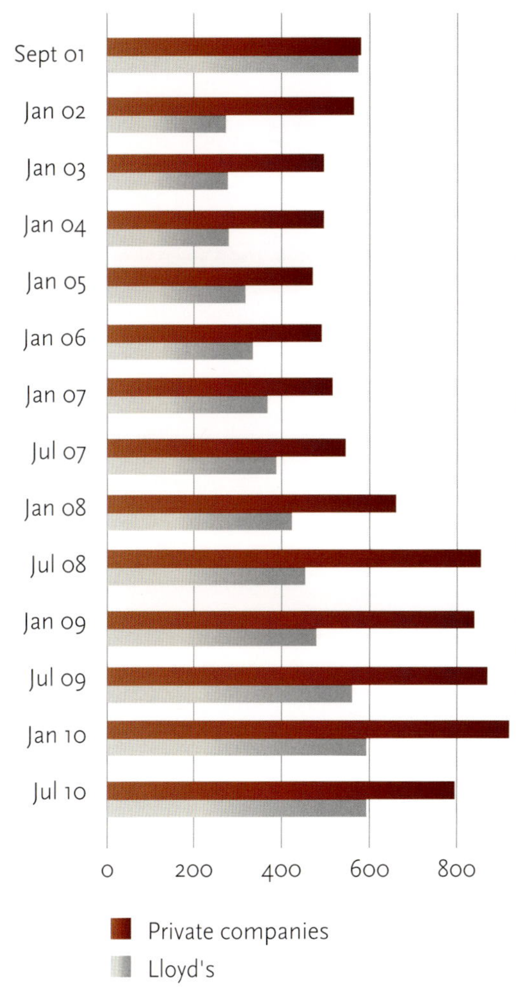

Source: Gallagher London.
Note: The private market total is lower than the sum of private companies' and Lloyd's capacity, because several providers are able to underwrite projects with either their companies' or Lloyd's lines and are counted in both.

Public and multilateral PRI providers do not appear to have modified their overall capacity either. BU members surveyed for this report indicated that they did not expect any changes in the near to medium term.

Given the lower level of new PRI contracts issued, the volume of overall capacity—both public and private—currently exceeds the level of demand. This finding could have implications both in terms of pricing and the cover offered, because investors may seek to negotiate more favorable conditions in their PRI contracts. At the same time, insurers do not expect any significant changes in the type and scope of coverage they are able to provide.

Although capacity is available, some PRI brokers report that, in practice, insurers' willingness to provide cover has declined in specific countries where political risk is perceived to have deteriorated.

Reinsurance

How much PRI providers are able to underwrite, in particular in the private segment of the market, is largely determined by the availability of reinsurance. The reinsurance market demonstrated its resilience during the worst of the financial crisis and has remained relatively stable. Although some reinsurers suffered losses during the crisis—particularly those with higher exposure to business lines relating to trade credit, structured finance, and credit default swaps—and reduced some lines as a result, those markets have begun to stabilize and show signs of positive growth. In addition, the PRI segment did not suffer similar loss levels, and reinsurers were able to keep their PRI offer relatively stable. Swiss Re, which had cut back its supply following significant losses incurred in non-PRI–related instruments, has now brought some of its reinsurance lines closer to pre-crisis levels.

PRI providers indeed report that they have been able to conclude the renewal of their reinsurance treaties without any significant change and are, therefore able to maintain the capacity they can offer to investors.

Claims

Unlike the trade credit and structured trade segments of the insurance markets, where claims in 2009 more than doubled compared to 2008, the PRI segment experienced few losses. BU members reported $24.2 million of claims in 2009—or only 3 percent of premium revenues, among the lowest levels in the last 15 years (figure 3.5).

Most of the losses in 2009 were relatively small, and recoveries have been significant at $9.5 million, resulting in lower levels of net losses. PRI, unlike trade credit insurance, does not cover commercial risk and, therefore, has not suffered losses due to defaults and non-payment resulting from the global downturn.

Although losses did spike somewhat in 2008—mainly due to one large claim in the Philippines—they were down significantly in 2009. At the same time, premium income continued to grow during the same period, in spite of the decline in new business and overall portfolio: BU members generated an estimated $955 million in premiums, an increase of about 12 percent from 2008.

This trend is expected to continue through 2010. Although claims spiked to more than $61 million in the first half of 2010, this amount was modest compared to premium earned. In addition, most of the losses suffered in 2010 were concentrated in one country (República Bolivariana de Venezuela) and were mainly caused by a single large expropriation.

Figure 3.5 Loss ratios

Percent of premium income

Source: Berne Union.

Global developments over the past few years have had an impact on PRI providers' political risk perceptions. Last year, a number of insurers expected that claims for expropriation and non-honoring of sovereign guarantees would rise over the next few years. Providers interviewed this year still believed that fiscal strains resulting from the impact of the global crisis and economic rescue packages, as well as the rise of resource nationalism in some regions, could translate into more losses in the future. However, it appears that such claims have not yet materialized on a large scale.

Pricing

Following the softening of PRI prices in the period 2004–2007, the PRI market hardened in the midst of the financial crisis. Following an increase in 2008, premiums continued to rise during 2009. As a result, BU members' revenues in 2009 were about 12 percent higher than in 2008, even though total exposure declined. As contracts with lower premium rates expired and were being replaced with new policies carrying higher prices, average premiums earned, which accounted for 0.6 percent of average maximum aggregate liability in 2008, increased slightly to 0.7 percent in 2009, equivalent to levels observed in 2006 (figure 3.6). Premiums seem to have stabilized during 2010 because insurers report no real increase in rates this year. With the weak real demand for PRI cover, rates may soften somewhat until an increase in the projects going through the complete underwriting cycle is realized.

Although some amount of innovation and product development has taken place within the PRI industry,[6] PRI remains a niche product covering a small percentage of FDI to developing countries. The nature of political risk is constantly evolving, sources of perils have multiplied, and the delineation between political and other risks is often blurred (chapter 1). As a result, some investors argue that the industry lags behind the fast-evolving nature of political risk and the ever more complex type of perils they face.[7] The PRI industry covers only part of the political perils that investors face in developing countries, and the gap is perhaps nowhere more pronounced than in CAF investment destinations.

Figure 3.6 Ratio of premiums to average maximum limit of liability for BU members

Percent

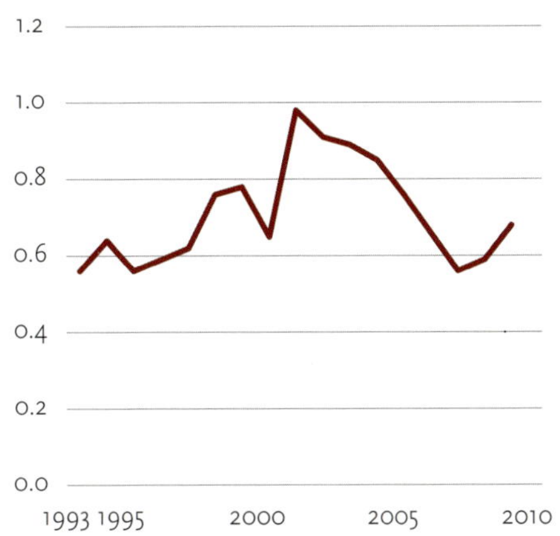

Source: Berne Union.

Political Risk Insurance in CAF Economies

Most investors involved in CAF countries surveyed for this report choose not to pursue PRI (chapter 2). Only 13 percent of respondents to the MIGA-EIU CAF Investors Survey reported seeking PRI, and fewer still ended up contracting it.

The main reasons cited for not using insurance are that potential losses are small or that risks are manageable without it (figure 3.7). This finding suggests PRI is a niche product used primarily to avoid catastrophic losses or is useful for certain types of risk. This use could also mean that investors involved in CAF countries may have a higher tolerance for risk or ability to manage it, that investments in those destinations tend to have quicker payback times or are smaller than in other developing countries, or both. This could also suggest that potential losses in these destinations are expected to be related to political violence, which typically are more contained than are those caused by expropriation or breach of contract. A significantly higher proportion of medium and large companies, as well as North-based investors, invoked the two main reasons for not using PRI compared to respondents from multinational enterprises (MNE) that were either smaller or were based in developing countries.

Consistent with these results, close to 90 percent of respondents said that whether PRI is available or not does not have influence on their decision to invest. This finding is consistent with the theme that PRI's interaction with the wide array of risk-mitigation tools available to investors is not well understood.

Small companies were marginally more likely than large ones to take PRI into account in their investment decisions. MNEs from developing countries were also four times more likely than were those from industrialized countries to reconsider their investment if insurance were not available.[8]

Figure 3.7 Main reasons for not using political risk insurance

Percent of respondents

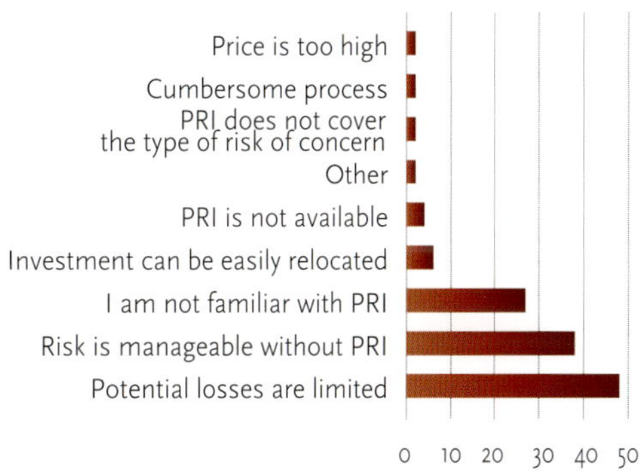

Source: MIGA-EIU CAF Investors Survey.

Similarly, about a third of investors in financial services say they would halt investments if insurance were not available, whereas no respondent in the primary sector would. This result is in line with last year's survey findings, which suggested that investors in financial services were the highest users of PRI in relative terms, whereas those in the primary sector were the least likely to rely on insurance. As noted earlier, investors in financial services often get provisioning relief[9] when obtaining political risk cover, which makes PRI particularly attractive. Investors in extractive industries, conversely, face more limited choices when it comes to investment destinations (chapter 2). Because investors often must operate in countries perceived as riskier, assessing and managing political risk has become part of their core business.

Although interest in insurance—or the lack of it—is related mainly to a perception that risk is manageable and losses are limited, about a quarter of respondents—whether North- or South-based—also reported that they are not familiar with PRI. This finding raises questions about the PRI industry's outreach and awareness-raising efforts, especially toward smaller firms, for which lack of familiarity appears more pronounced.

At the same time, a significant minority of investors—particularly those from developing countries—reported shortcomings in supply: insurance either was not available, did not cover desired risks, was considered prohibitively expensive, or was too cumbersome to obtain (figure 3.7). Insurers often perceive CAF countries as riskier, and cover for these destinations, although available, appears relatively limited.

Multilateral PRI providers, which are in a better position to provide cover in investment destinations considered riskier, can play a catalyst role and can expand market capacity for these destinations by generating reinsurance and coinsurance from other PRI providers (see the section on multilateral initiatives). Yet, the impact of PRI on its own is limited: the political and security situation, as well as business opportunities, weigh far more heavily on investors' interest and risk appetite. Indeed, the main reasons surveyed investors were not deterred was that they consider that business opportunities in the CAF countries where they invest outweigh political risks, and that risks are perceived as manageable. These results were consistent regardless of investors' sectors, company size, or geographical origin. Until conflicts are resolved, short-term trade transactions and local investment are likely to dominate.

PRI Supply: A Market Failure?

Although CAF countries attracted about 6.2 percent of FDI flowing into the developing world during 2005–2009 (chapter 2), they accounted for 10 percent of new investment PRI underwritten by BU members[10] over the same period. Yet, new PRI business in CAF countries shrank by over 21 percent in 2009, while FDI to these destinations declined by 13 percent. The decline in new PRI business for investment in all developing countries was even more pronounced (38.5 percent), but it was largely in line with the 40 percent decline in FDI flows to developing countries. In the first half of 2010, however, $4.9 billion worth of new business was underwritten in CAF countries—more than in the full year of 2009 and close to 18 percent of the BU's new business—mainly because of large transactions in Myanmar and Papua New Guinea.

The BU reports outstanding PRI cover in almost all CAF countries. Yet, insurance is heavily concentrated in a handful of resource-rich investment destinations, which absorb over 60 percent of the exposure.

Similarly, most PRI coverage in CAF countries has been underwritten by a relatively small number of BU members: five private insurers have accounted for over half of the BU's outstanding portfolio in CAF countries over the past five years—significantly higher than their 35 percent of the BU's maximum limit of liabilities for all developing countries. Although the bulk of private PRI by value is concentrated in resource-rich countries, the outstanding portfolio includes a wide range of CAF investment destinations. Most of the cover in CAF countries, whether resource dependent or not, appears to be concentrated in activities related to the extractive and energy sectors, which offer attractive opportunities for private PRI providers. In some cases, the involvement of these private PRI providers in a wide range of CAF countries also reflects, although to a much lesser extent, their ability to offer worldwide or multicountry PRI policies and, therefore, to underwrite cover in riskier countries as part of a broader package.

Over the same period of time, public PRI providers accounted for only 39 percent of the BU's outstanding portfolio in CAF countries, the bulk of which was underwritten by only four insurers: KEIC (Republic of Korea), NEXI (Japan), OPIC (United States), and Sinosure (China). A number of ECAs rely on ratings compiled under the umbrella of the Organisation for Economic Co-operation and Development (OECD) (box 3.4) to determine availability, cover, and pricing for investment insurance. As of July 2010, the overwhelming majority of CAF countries was assigned the riskiest rating or not rated at all,[11] resulting in scant PRI availability. Following sovereign debt relief provided to low-income countries, many of which are considered fragile or affected by conflict (chapter 2), ECAs have also committed to ensure that the provision of official export credits to public or publicly guaranteed buyers in these countries should reflect sustainable lending practices (box 3.5).[12] As a result, ECAs' provision of PRI for the non-honoring of sovereign guarantees for CAF countries has been subject to added scrutiny.

PRI providers surveyed for this report say they receive demands for insurance in CAF countries; private insurers, in particular, appear to be solicited for a much broader range of destinations than ECAs. Supply, however, appears to be falling short. As noted earlier, a substantial minority of investors involved in CAF countries and surveyed for this report argue that they do not rely on PRI because it is not available, is inadequate, or is too expensive. A quarter of respondents involved in CAF countries also reported they were not familiar with PRI.

Most ECAs are either off cover for CAF investment destinations, or they offer highly restrictive cover. The main reasons cited are risk, OECD ratings, and foreign policy considerations (such as official sanctions or embargoes).

However, private providers appear more nimble and willing to consider cover on a case-by-case basis, according to their own risk assessment, investors' experience, and sectors involved. Previous claims, whether on the insurance or export credit side, do not in themselves seem to weigh heavily on the investment insurance decisions. Some products offered on the private market—such as worldwide or multicountry insurance policies—also allow private insurers to bundle riskier underwriting. Private insurers report that reinsurance is available for CAF countries and usually not a constraint, even if amounts are limited. When insurance is offered, however, conditions and carve-outs are often very restrictive.

Box 3.4 OECD Country Risk Ratings

OECD country ratings are designed to set guidelines to price the default risk on export credit and to set minimum premium rates charged by participating ECAs. The ratings came into effect in 1999 as part of rules known as the Knaepen Package,[a] which is integrated into an arrangement seeking to create a level playing field for official support of export credits and encourage the convergence of premium rates.[b] The ratings provide a system that classifies countries into eight categories, ranging from zero (least risky) to seven (riskiest).

The rating primarily assesses the ability of a country to service its external debt. It is based on two components: (i) a quantitative model of country credit risk that is based on payment experience and on the country's financial and economic situation, and (ii) a qualitative assessment that seeks to integrate relevant elements not quantified into the model, such as political factors. The final classification is reached by consensus of country risk experts from participating ECAs, and ratings are reviewed at least once a year. Participating ECAs are from Australia, Canada, the European Union member countries, Japan, the Republic of Korea, New Zealand, Norway, Switzerland, and the United States.[c]

Although the ratings were created to price export credit insurance, they are also taken into account for the underwriting of investment insurance.

a OECD, *Minimum Risk Premium: the Knaepen Package.* (http://www.oecd.org/document/34/0,3343,en_2649_34171_1830178_1_1_1_1,00.html).

b OECD *Arrangement on Officially Supported Export Credits*, January 2010 Revision. (http://www.oecd.org/officialdocuments/displaydocumentpdf/?cote=TAD/PG(2010)2&doclanguage=en).

c See the OECD website for the full list of participating ECAs. (http://www.oecd.org/countrylist/0,3349,en_2649_34169_1783635_1_1_1_37431,00.html).

Multilateral and regional insurers, as required by their developmental mandate, are in principle more amenable to consider cover in investment destinations considered difficult. Because of their ownership structure, they are in a better negotiating position than is the private market to avert potential claims caused by government intervention, or to recover losses from host countries' authorities when such a claim has occurred. Member countries of the African Trade Insurance Agency (ATI), for instance, are legally required to reimburse any claims paid by the agency except those arising from political violence. Multilateral insurers, however, are bound by their country membership and a limited product range, as well as their own risk assessments.

Risk perception, therefore, remains a significant obstacle. When the potential for loss is too high or is deemed inevitable, the risk is considered uninsurable.

While CAF countries have been responsible for 60 percent of the value of BU's claims since 1990, this is due primarily to two very large losses related to wars in the Persian Gulf and the Balkans. Without taking into account these two claims, claims related to CAF countries have accounted for about 13 percent of all BU claims over the same period.

Over the past five years, however, CAF countries have not appeared to generate significantly more claims than other developing investment destinations. CAF countries are responsible for 9.6 percent of claims paid by BU members since 2005—in line with their average share of new business (10 percent), and only slightly above their portion of maximum liability (7.7 percent) over the same period. The ratio of recovery for claims paid in CAF countries over the past five years (58.2 percent) is also broadly in line with what has been observed in other developing countries (62.4 percent).

Box 3.5 The Nonconcessional Borrowing Policy

To avoid the re-accumulation of external debt in low-income countries having benefited from Multilateral Debt Relief Initiative, the World Bank's International Development Association (IDA) introduced the nonconcessional borrowing policy (NCBP) in July 2006, which was updated in April 2010. The policy is meant to promote financing of low-income countries on concessional terms by encouraging creditors to take into account debt sustainability in their lending decisions, as well as establishing minimum grant elements for future borrowing from IDA countries.

As a result, an increased number of creditors are committed to adhering to the NCBP. The OECD Working Group on ECAs, for instance, has adopted a set of guidelines discouraging the provision of official export credits for expenditures considered unproductive, and ensuring that minimum IDA concessionality requirements are observed. The guidelines also require members to report details of official export credit transactions to IDA countries and to review them on an annual basis.

Sources: World Bank, 2010, IDA's *Non-Concessional Borrowing Policy: Progress Update*, April 2010, Washington, DC: World Bank; International Monetary Fund, 2010, "Concessionality and the Design of Debt Limits in IMF-Supported Programs in Low-Income Countries" (last updated in March 2010). http://www.imf.org/external/np/pdr/conc/index.htm.

The claims profile for CAF countries seems indeed vastly different from the rest of the developing world. These countries account for 78 percent of BU claims paid for losses caused by political violence over the past five years. However, they contributed a minuscule proportion of losses caused by expropriation—which accounts for the largest share of BU members' total claim payments with almost 60 percent.

These five-year averages mask substantial annual swings. While losses in 2005–2007 were responsible for a deterioration of CAF ratios, no claims were paid for these countries in 2008 and 2009 (figures 3.8 and 3.9).

In addition, losses over the past five years have been concentrated in only five countries. The number of claims has also been small, with one large claim for breach of contract in 2006 heavily tilting the balance.

Figure 3.8 Claims paid by BU members

$ million

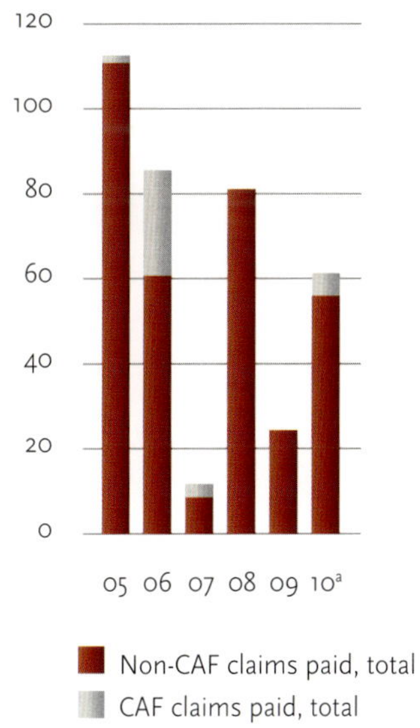

Source: Berne Union.
Note: a= First half.

Although losses caused by political violence have been more frequent than any other losses in CAF countries, payments have been small in absolute terms: $2.1 million out of a total of $36.1 million for the past five years. Losses related to this type of political risk are often partial; expropriation and breach of contract, however, can wipe out entire investments and often result in much larger claims. Claims paid for political violence losses, moreover, are far more difficult to recover than those related to government intervention, because responsibility is difficult to assign.

Figure 3.9 Claims paid for losses caused by political violence by BU members

$ million

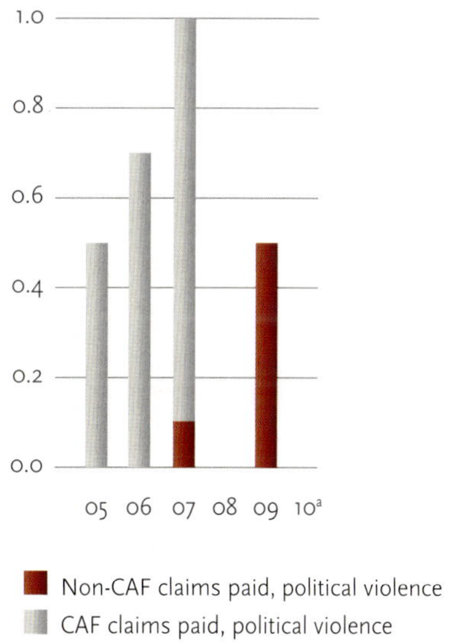

Source: Berne Union.
Note: a= First half.

Multilateral CAF Initiatives: Rising to the Challenge

Given most fragile countries' limited local savings capacity and ability to tap into international financial markets, FDI is a critical component of private sector development and economic growth in these economies (chapter 2). Yet, most CAF countries—especially those poorly endowed in natural resources—struggle to attract foreign investment (chapter 2). As highlighted in the previous chapter, part of the problem is the level of perceived political risk. Although PRI cannot in itself generate FDI, it can in some cases encourage it and, therefore, contribute to economic recovery in CAF countries.

Given the limitations of the PRI industry highlighted earlier in this chapter, a number of initiatives have sought to fill the gap not only by directly covering FDI inflows into CAF countries, but also by generating more PRI capacity in the rest of the market through coinsurance and reinsurance. The multilateral nature of these initiatives, which as noted earlier provides some deterrence against adverse government intervention, has helped convince other PRI providers to join in and extend cover for investments in destinations they may not have otherwise considered. A selection of such initiatives is highlighted next.

The African Trade Insurance Agency (ATI)

ATI was created to address a market in risk-mitigation products in Africa. Launched in 2001, the agency provides insurance and reinsurance for both investment and trade related to African member countries.[13] Since its inception, ATI has supported over $2.1 billion worth of trade and investments across the region. Although the initiative was not specifically designed to focus on CAF countries, a substantial portion of ATI's PRI portfolio has been underwritten for projects in its more volatile members, covering all perils. ATI has successfully helped create additional insurance capacity for these countries through reinsurance arrangements, in particular with Lloyd's. Insurance partners have been particularly keen to get involved in reconstruction projects, which often involve support from donors or development financial institutions and are, therefore, perceived to provide additional deterrence against adverse government interventions. More recently, ATI also started offering reinsurance to commercial insurers in East Africa, allowing them to offer property cover against damage caused by political violence, terrorism, and sabotage. The agency reports that although African investors tend to have lower risk perceptions than those from industrialized countries, when it comes to projects on the continent, they face higher hurdles mobilizing finance for these projects.

Within ATI's first three years of operation, demand for insurance in Burundi had outstripped the agency's capacity. More funding had to be raised to expand the agency's ability to provide cover. Much of the portfolio has been concentrated in construction, telecoms, and manufacturing, and no claim has been recorded so far. Burundi accounts for 3.7 percent of ATI's gross PRI portfolio.

The Democratic Republic of Congo, however, accounts for over one-third (38.7 percent) of ATI's gross PRI exposure, in spite of the country's long history of political and economic instability, as well as its devastating civil war. ATI has been very successful in mobilizing reinsurance for investments in the Democratic Republic of Congo, and most of its gross portfolio has been ceded to other PRI providers. Although most of the PRI underwritten is concentrated in the mining sector, the agency has also supported projects in construction and information technology (IT). As a result of escalating risks, in particular in extractive industries, ATI's premiums in the Democratic Republic of Congo have risen by about 40 percent since 2009,[14] and longer tenors have become more difficult to obtain. Although no PRI claim has yet been paid, a request for compensation has been presented for a mining project.

ATI's presence on the ground in both countries facilitates risk assessments, as well as claim prevention. The agency is currently seeking approval to increase its project and country limits.

The Islamic Corporation for Insurance of Investment and Export Credit (ICIEC)

ICIEC was established in August 1994 to boost economic ties among Islamic countries. A subsidiary of the Islamic Development Bank, ICIEC now has 40 member countries in the Middle East, Africa, Asia, and Europe. Eleven ICIEC member countries are considered CAF for the purposes of this report, and they account for over half of ICIEC's total outstanding portfolio for PRI.

Most of ICIEC's insurance underwritten in the countries that form the basis of the analysis presented in this report is concentrated in Sudan, the Islamic Republic of Iran, Pakistan, and the Republic of Yemen. Demand for cover in these countries has been on the rise, reflecting both increased investment and trade flows, as well as heightened risk aversion. Most of ICIEC's capacity in the Islamic Republic of Iran and Sudan has already been utilized for trade transactions, however, leaving little spare capacity for investment PRI. At the same time, there has been very little or no demand for other CAF countries.

Obtaining reinsurance for CAF countries, such as the Islamic Republic of Iran and Sudan, has been increasingly difficult, limiting ICIEC's ability to meet insurance demand for investments over its $81 million project limit. In addition, although ICIEC provides all kinds of cover for CAF countries, restrictions may apply in some cases, in particular when it comes to war and civil disturbance. For instance, ICIEC may not offer insurance against political violence in regions considered high risk. Prices also reflect the perceived higher risk.

Projects in Sudan generate the most demand by far, accounting for 28 percent of ICIEC's total exposure.[15] Insurance has sometimes been a necessary condition for projects to go forward, even for investors and financiers from the Gulf, whose perception of political risk in Sudan is usually lower than those from industrialized countries (box 3.6). ICIEC has reached its capacity ceiling for both Sudan and the Islamic Republic of Iran, but attempts to establish special funds to expand PRI supply in view of growing demand have been unsuccessful, due to the global financial crisis and international sanctions.

So far, ICIEC has not received any claim in its investment insurance operations.

The Multilateral Investment Guarantee Agency (MIGA)

Besides directly covering CAF countries that are members, MIGA has been involved in a number of special initiatives:

EU Investment Trust Fund for Bosnia and Herzegovina

With the war that ravaged the country ending in 1995, developed countries were keen to support the reconstruction of Bosnia and Herzegovina and to prevent a return to conflict. NATO troops were stationed in the country, and foreign assistance poured in.

In 1997, the European Commission, in partnership with MIGA, established a $12 million investment guarantee trust fund to support a resumption of FDI in the country. A presence on the ground greatly helped promote the fund's services with potential investors and assess risks. Some European ECAs did not cover Bosnia and Herzegovina, prompting investors to turn to the fund.

The fund was fully utilized, issuing PRI for projects such as the establishment of a dialysis clinic in Banja Luka and the expansion of a soft drink plant. Most of the investments covered, however, were in

Box 3.6 Oil Exploration Project in Sudan

In 2005, a midsized Emirati oil and gas company was awarded a contract to undertake oil exploration for a local joint venture company owned by the China National Petroleum Corporation, Petronas of Malaysia, and the government of Sudan. Three Gulf Banks, one from Saudi Arabia and two from the United Arab Emirates, agreed to finance the $14.2 million project, but only on the condition that they could obtain political risk insurance.

The three banks approached ICIEC, which provided the needed cover against the risks of transfer restrictions, expropriation, and war and civil disturbance. The project was located at Adrael near Malakal in southern Sudan, a region with a history of long-running conflict with northern Sudan. Thanks to ICIEC's insurance, the banks funded the project, and the loans were repaid without any incident or claim. The project created many jobs in a country that has been through the longest running armed conflicts in Africa.

Source: ICIEC.

financial services, because foreign banks were keen to establish branches in Bosnia and Herzegovina and were one of the largest sources of FDI. In addition, the fund generated additional capacity through co-insurance and reinsurance with other PRI providers.

FDI to Bosnia and Herzegovina ballooned from $1 million in 1997 to $177 million in 1999 and $710 million in 2004.[16] A number of factors combined to attract foreign investors. The heavy presence of NATO troops in a relatively small country mitigated the risk of a return to conflict. Bosnia and Herzegovina's economy was relatively well developed and offered promising business prospects. In the heart of Europe, the country was also a familiar environment for most investors in the immediate region. In addition, banking reform introduced became instrumental in attracting foreign investment in financial services. Investment in other sectors did not enjoy the same advantages, however, and were much

Box 3.7 Supporting Local SMEs in the West Bank and Gaza

The European Palestinian Credit Guarantee Fund (EPCGF)—sponsored by the German Financial Cooperation, the German bank KfW under mandate from the European Commission, and the European Investment Bank—was created to stimulate lending to local small and medium-size enterprises (SME), which face substantial liquidity problems. The facility backs five-year loans of up to $100,000 provided through eight local banks to companies with fewer than 20 employees. The guarantee covers 60 percent of the amount borrowed. Since it was launched in late 2005, the credit guarantee fund's local partner banks have extended around 900 loans worth over $26 million.

In July 2007, the Middle East Investment Initiative (MEII), a nonprofit organization that partners with private and public entities to offer specialized financial products, launched a $160 million loan guarantee facility focused primarily on Palestinian SMEs, which compose nearly 90 percent of all Palestinian businesses. Local lending to SMEs had become virtually non-existent because of the risk of default. The facility supports lending through local banks by providing guarantees of up to 70 percent of loan amounts. This facility is transforming traditional Palestinian lending practices from a collateral-based system (sometimes as high as 200 percent of the loan amount) to one based on cash flow. The program was set up in partnership with the Overseas Private Investment Corporation (OPIC)—the U.S. agency that facilitates US private investment in developing countries—and the Palestine Investment Fund (PIF). MEII works with CHF International, an aid agency, in providing training and technical assistance to local bank managers and loan officers to improve and expand lending services. So far, more than 300 loans worth more than $60 million have been guaranteed.

Palestinian banking officials and local business leaders also expressed interest in insurance for local businesses against trade disruption and political violence. MEII is now developing a new political risk insurance facility, in cooperation with OPIC and the Ramallah-based National Insurance Company (NIC). The facility, primarily targeting Palestinian exporters, would insure against losses resulting from trade disruption caused by border closing or delays, as well as asset damage resulting from political violence. Besides technical assistance, OPIC and MEII would provide NIC with more than $1 million in reinsurance. Now in the pilot stage, the Palestinian Political Risk Insurance is expected to launch in 2011.

Sources: KfW, MEII, and OPIC.

slower to develop, butting against weak business laws, a divided country, and a local government that was barely functioning.

In 2007—over a decade after the conflict ended—Bosnia and Herzegovina attracted over $2 billion in FDI, equivalent to 14 percent of its GDP.[17]

The West Bank and Gaza Investment Guarantee Trust Fund

The political trajectory in the West Bank and Gaza has been disappointing for investors. The West Bank and Gaza Investment Guarantee Trust Fund was created in 1997, when the Oslo agreement seemed to herald a resolution to the political crisis in the region. The trust fund became operational in 1998, with a $20 million capacity financed by the Palestinian Authority (with an IDA grant), the European Investment Bank, and the Japanese authorities.

The fund underwrote only one tourism investment in 1999 for $5 million; the policy was canceled the following year. The political situation in the region deteriorated significantly from 2000 onward. As a result, foreign investors' interest in the small economy waned, FDI flows declined from $218 million in 1998 to $9 million in 2002,[18] and preliminary applications for PRI from the trust fund evaporated. Attempts to harness reinsurance and coinsurance were unsuccessful. Although FDI somewhat recovered in 2004–2005, it plummeted once again in 2006 because of political developments, and it still remains well below levels observed in the late 1990s.

In 2008, the fund expanded its reach to include local investors, a broader range of debt, and existing investments. The modification appears to have had little impact on demand for cover: local investors' main worry when it comes to political risk is business interruption for periods of 2–5 days, which is significantly shorter than those covered by the fund (30 days). In addition, many local investments are on a very small scale, making PRI relatively less attractive and more cumbersome.

A presence on the ground, which proved so crucial in other initiatives (see earlier), has now been established to explore better ways to tailor the fund's services to local needs. In addition, a business development plan has been formulated for the facility, and a public awareness campaign has been initiated. These efforts appear to be bearing fruit: by the end of September 2010, six applications had been received for both new and expansion investments.

Non-MIGA initiatives in the West Bank and Gaza focusing on local lending and credit guarantees, rather than on foreign investors, have been more successful (box 3.7).

The Afghanistan Investment Guarantee Facility

The $12 million Afghanistan Investment Guarantee Facility—sponsored by the Afghan government (through an IDA grant), the UK Department for International Development, and the Asian Development Bank—was created in 2005. From inception, the facility was designed to heavily leverage its own capacity to generate additional cover from the PRI market through coinsurance and reinsurance.

So far, the fund has underwritten $3.5 million worth of cover for six investments—including a $60 million telecom deal and six small projects—resulting in total cover of $107 million after reinsurance and coinsurance, from both MIGA's own account and the private market. One claim related to the war and civil disturbance cover has been received and is currently being evaluated.

Activity has significantly slowed down in the past few years, however, because of a deterioration of the political and security situation in Afghanistan. In 2009, the number of preliminary applications was less than a third of those received in 2006. Activities are still ongoing, however, and MIGA has received applications for an infrastructure expansion project and a greenfield investment in agribusiness.

The CAF States Facility

To further encourage economic activity in CAF countries, MIGA is working to establish a multi-country facility offering PRI for both trade and investment. The facility will be structured as a public-private partnership with a total insurance capacity of $500 million. Though the project is still in its initial stages, MIGA hopes to launch the facility in 2011.

Conclusion

Although modest, the anticipated rebound in FDI flows, added to the growing weight of the developing world as an investment destination and to persistent concerns over political risk in developing countries from both North- and South-based investors, bode well for PRI providers. The PRI industry on the whole remained largely stable throughout the crisis, and prospects for a rebound in new business appear promising for 2010 and beyond, as credit constraints ease further and FDI recovers.

Yet, PRI is likely to remain a niche product among risk-mitigation techniques. In the short term, concerns over the pace and sustainability of the global economic recovery dominate. The onset of the global crisis and the constant evolution of political perils do not appear to have resulted in heavier reliance on insurance, even though investors in both developing and CAF economies are most concerned about adverse government interventions. Although PRI has a role to play in fostering investment in CAF states by mitigating some political risks, other factors such as business opportunities, market size, and reform in these countries weigh heavily on investment decisions.

The low ratio of FDI to GDP in CAF economies is in line with their economic weight. PRI, although unlikely in itself to significantly increase investment flows, can potentially help diversify FDI flows to these countries beyond the extractive industry. Provided the business environment is supportive, the availability of PRI is more likely to make a difference for investments in sectors more prone to be deterred by conflict and fragility, such as financial services. Yet, a significant minority of investors report either that they are not familiar with PRI, or that available stand-alone PRI products are inadequate.

In a context of constantly changing political risks, the PRI industry needs to keep evolving to remain relevant. Although traditional cover remains pertinent as perils such as resource nationalism, fiscal imbalances, or exchange rate tensions reappear, the emergence of new perils, as well as persisting concerns over political risks usually not covered by insurance, also require constant innovation. In CAF countries, where economic recovery often holds the key to future stability and where FDI plays an even greater role given the dearth of other sources of private capital, multilateral PRI providers have a unique role to play mobilizing supply and adjusting products to these economies' specific needs.

Chapter three—endnotes

1 PRI refers to a broad range of product lines that include both trade credit and investment insurance. For this report, any reference to PRI applies exclusively to investment insurance. See box 3.3 on the benefits of PRI for investors.

2 Because Lloyd's syndicates do not publish PRI data, quantitative industry trends were largely extrapolated from data published by the BU, the association of public and private sector providers of export credit and investment insurance, and Gallagher London (an insurance broker). To complement its market analysis for this chapter, MIGA surveyed private PRI providers from the London market through a roundtable discussion organized in May 2010, questionnaires, and interviews. Findings from this exercise have been taken into account to complement market trends suggested by BU and Gallagher London data.

3 See MIGA, 2009, *World Investment and Political Risk 2009*, Washington, DC: World Bank for more details on the relationship between FDI and PRI.

4 Gallagher London, July 2010, *Political Risk Insurance (PRI), Report and Market Update*, London: Gallagher.

5 Ibid.

6 Raoul Ascari, 2010, "Political Risk Insurance: An Industry in Search of a Business?" Working Paper No. 12, SACE, March.

7 Patrick Garver, 2009, "The Changing Face of Political Risk," in Kevin W. Lu, Gero Verheyen, and Srilal M. Perera, eds., *Investing with Confidence, Understanding Political Risk Management in the 21st Century*, Washington, DC: World Bank, 81.

8 The MIGA-EIU CAF Investors Survey did not investigate whether answers might change should comprehensive coverage be offered.

9 PRI allows financial institutions, in some jurisdictions, to utilize the insurers credit for loan-loss provisioning purposes rather than the country-specific provisioning requirement, resulting in overall lower levels of provisions.

10 Kosovo is not included in BU data.

11 OECD, 2010, Country Risk Classifications of the Participants to the Arrangement on Officially Supported Export Credit, July 2. http://www.oecd.org/dataoecd/47/29/3782900.pdf.

12 OECD, 2008, Principles and Guidelines to Promote Sustainable Lending Practices in the Provision of Official Export Credit to Low Income Countries, May 22. http://www.oecd.org/officialdocuments/displaydocumentpdf/?cote=TAD/ECG(2008)15&doclanguage=en.

13 Full member states include Burundi, the Democratic Republic of Congo, Kenya, Madagascar, Malawi, Rwanda, Tanzania, Uganda, and Zambia. In addition, Benin, Côte d'Ivoire, Djibouti, Eritrea, Gabon, Ghana, Liberia, and Sudan are in the process of completing their memberships.

14 "Mine Dispute, Poll Fears Raise Congo Risk Premiums," Reuters, May 18, 2010. http://www.miningweekly.com/article/mine-dispute-poll-fears-raise-congo-risk-premiums-2010-05-18.

15 Both trade and investment insurance.

16 World Bank estimates.

17 Ibid.

18 Ibid.

APPENDICES

Appendix 1 FDI Inflows, 2002–2009

$ billion

	2002	2003	2004	2005	2006	2007	2008	2009[e]
World	738	639	741	1,126	1,484	2,301	1,832	1,085
Developed countries	583	487	535	852	1,141	1,793	1,245	731
Developing countries	154	152	207	274	343	508	587	354
Latin America and the Carribbean	57.4	43.3	65.9	72.2	72.0	109.4	127.9	73.6
Argentina	2.15	1.65	4.12	5.27	5.54	6.47	9.73	4.01
Brazil	16.59	10.14	18.17	15.07	18.78	34.58	45.06	25.95
Chile	2.55	4.31	7.17	6.98	7.30	12.53	15.18	12.70
Colombia	2.13	1.72	3.02	10.25	6.66	9.05	10.60	7.26
Costa Rica	0.66	0.58	0.79	0.86	1.47	1.90	2.02	1.32
Dominican Republic	0.92	0.61	0.91	1.12	1.53	1.58	2.88	2.16
Jamaica	0.48	0.72	0.60	0.68	0.88	0.87	1.44	1.06
Mexico	23.63	16.59	23.82	22.34	19.78	27.31	23.17	11.42
Peru	2.16	1.34	1.60	2.58	3.47	5.49	6.92	4.76
Uruguay	0.19	0.42	0.33	0.85	1.49	1.32	2.21	1.14
Venezuela, R.B.	0.78	2.04	1.48	2.60	(0.51)	1.01	0.35	(3.11)
East Asia and the Pacific	65.1	56.8	70.4	104.4	105.8	177.2	186.7	102.5
China	49.31	47.08	54.94	79.13	78.09	138.41	147.79	78.19
Indonesia	0.15	(0.60)	1.90	8.34	4.91	6.93	9.32	4.88
Malaysia	3.20	2.47	4.62	3.97	6.08	8.45	7.38	1.47
Philippines	1.54	0.49	0.69	1.85	2.92	2.92	1.54	1.95
Thailand	3.34	5.23	5.86	8.06	9.45	11.32	8.57	5.96
Vietnam	1.40	1.45	1.61	1.95	2.40	6.70	9.58	7.60
South Asia	1.4	5.4	7.8	11.2	26.0	32.3	48.7	38.3
Bangladesh	0.05	0.27	0.45	0.81	0.70	0.65	1.01	0.67
India	5.63	4.32	5.77	7.61	20.34	25.13	41.17	34.58
Pakistan	0.82	0.53	1.12	2.20	4.27	5.59	5.44	2.38
Sri Lanka	1.48	0.78	0.70	6.52	0.18)	5.74	9.64	5.63
Europa and Central Asia	10.3	22.4	40.9	49.2	87.5	130.0	157.4	83.4
Belarus	0.25	0.17	0.16	0.31	0.35	1.79	2.16	1.86
Bosnia and Herzegovina	0.27	0.38	0.71	0.61	0.72	2.07	1.06	0.51
Bulgaria	0.90	2.10	2.66	4.31	7.76	13.21	9.94	4.49
Kazakhstan	2.59	2.09	4.16	1.97	6.28	11.12	15.78	12.60
Romania	1.14	1.84	6.44	6.48	11.39	9.93	13.88	6.76
Russian Federation	3.46	7.96	15.44	12.89	29.70	55.07	75.00	37.13
Turkey	1.08	1.70	2.79	10.03	20.19	22.05	18.27	7.96
Ukraine	0.69	1.42	1.72	7.81	5.60	9.89	10.91	4.82

Appendix 1 FDI Inflows, 2002–2009 (cont'd)

$ billion

	2002	2003	2004	2005	2006	2007	2008	2009[e]
Middle East and North America	4.3	10.0	9.7	16.8	27.2	27.6	29.3	24.4
Algeria	1.07	0.63	0.88	1.08	1.80	1.66	2.65	2.31
Egypt, Arab Rep.	0.65	0.24	1.25	5.38	10.04	11.58	9.49	6.71
Iran, Islamic Rep.	0.55	0.48	0.31	0.92	0.32	1.66	1.49	3.02
Jordan	0.24	0.55	0.94	1.98	3.54	2.62	2.83	2.38
Lebanon	1.34	2.86	1.90	2.62	2.67	3.38	4.33	4.80
Morocco	0.08	2.31	0.79	1.62	2.37	2.81	2.47	1.33
Syrian Arab Republic	0.12	0.16	0.28	0.50	0.66	1.24	1.47	1.43
Tunisia	0.82	0.59	0.64	0.72	3.27	1.53	2.64	1.69
Sub-Saharan Africa	15.7	14.6	12.0	19.9	24.9	31.6	37.2	31.9
Angola	1.67	3.50	1.45	(1.30)	(0.04)	0.89)	1.68	2.21
Botswana	0.39	0.42	0.39	0.28	0.49	0.65	0.11	0.23
Congo, Dem. Rep.	0.14	0.32	0.01	(0.08)	(0.12)	0.72	1.00	0.95
Congo, Rep.	0.33	0.32	(0.01)	0.51	1.49	2.64	2.62	2.08
Ghana	0.06	0.14	0.14	0.14	0.64	0.97	2.11	1.68
Liberia	0.00	0.37	0.08	0.08	0.11	0.13	0.14	0.38
Madagascar	0.01	0.01	0.05	0.09	0.29	0.78	1.48	0.54
Mauritius	0.03	0.06	0.01	0.04	0.11	0.34	0.38	0.26
Mozambique	0.35	0.34	0.24	0.11	0.15	0.43	0.59	0.88
Niger	0.00	0.01	0.03	0.04	0.05	0.13	0.15	0.74
Nigeria	1.87	2.01	1.87	4.98	4.85	6.03	4.88	5.85
Seychelles	0.14	1.36	0.97	1.61	4.50	3.45	2.99	1.92
South Africa	0.00	(0.00)	(0.00)	0.02	0.10	0.14	0.09	0.11
Sudan	0.03	0.06	0.07	0.04	0.11	0.13	0.16	0.11
Swaziland	0.71	1.35	1.51	2.30	3.53	2.43	2.60	2.92
Uganda	0.18	0.20	0.30	0.38	0.64	0.79	0.81	0.60
Zambia	0.30	0.35	0.36	0.36	0.62	1.32	0.94	0.70

Source: World Bank estimates.
Note: Figures in parentheses represent negative numbers; e=estimate.

Appendix 2 MIGA-EIU Political Risk Survey 2010

The data provided herein are based on a survey conducted on behalf of the Multilateral Investment Guarantee Agency (MIGA) by the Economist Intelligence Unit (EIU). The survey was conducted in June 2010, and it contains the responses of 194 executives from multinational enterprises investing in developing countries, 55 percent of which were also represented in last year's survey. Quota sampling was used to ensure that the industry and geographic composition of the survey sample approximate the composition of actual FDI outflows to developing countries: following a first round of responses to the questionnaire, additional e-mail campaigns targeting respondents in specific sectors or locations were conducted until all demographic quotas were met.

Figure A2.1 What is your industry sector?

Percent of respondents

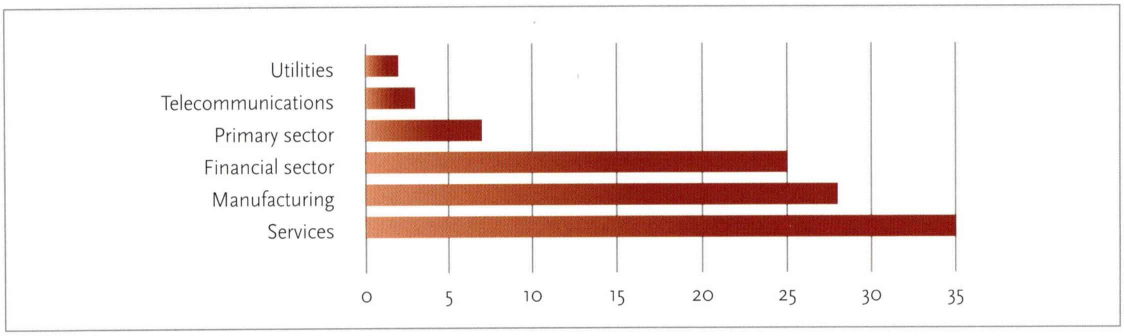

Figure A2.2 What are your organization's global annual revenues?

Percent of respondents

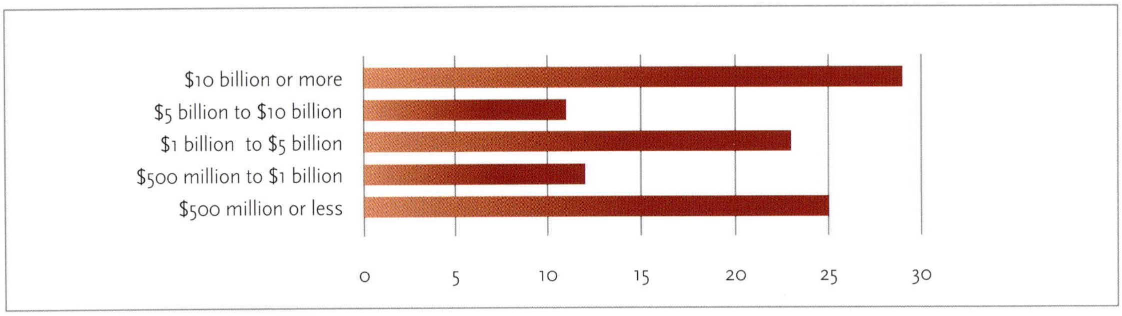

Figure A2.3 In which region is your company headquarters located?

Number of respondents

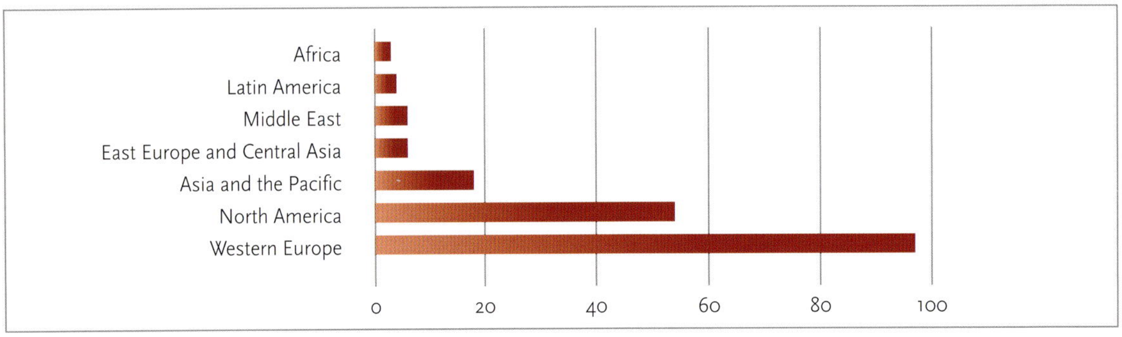

QUESTION 1. IN WHICH DEVELOPING COUNTRIES IS YOUR FIRM PRESENTLY INVESTING? SELECT ALL THAT APPLY.

Percent of respondents

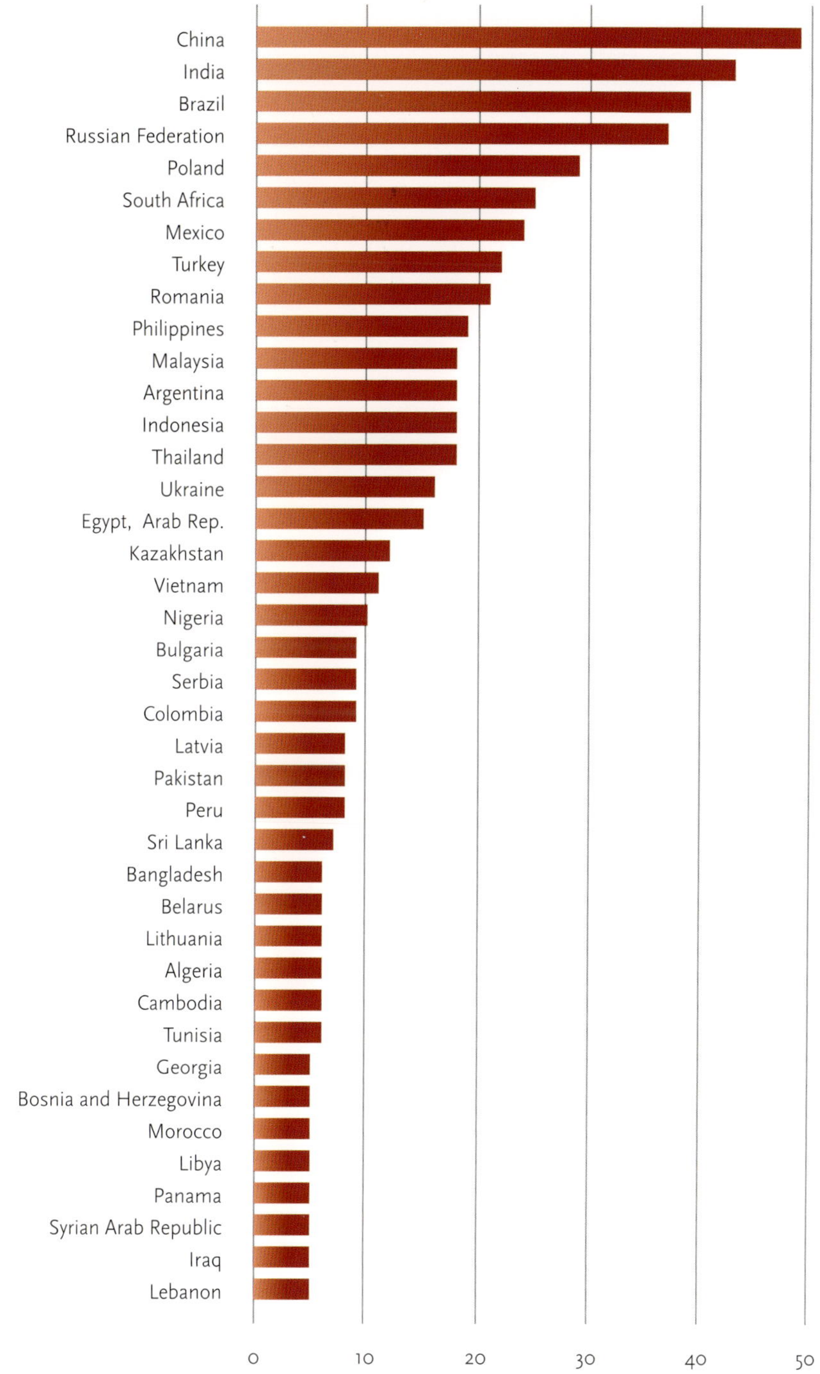

Question 2. How do you expect your company's planned investments abroad to change this year compared with last year and over the next three years compared with the previous three years?

Percent of respondents

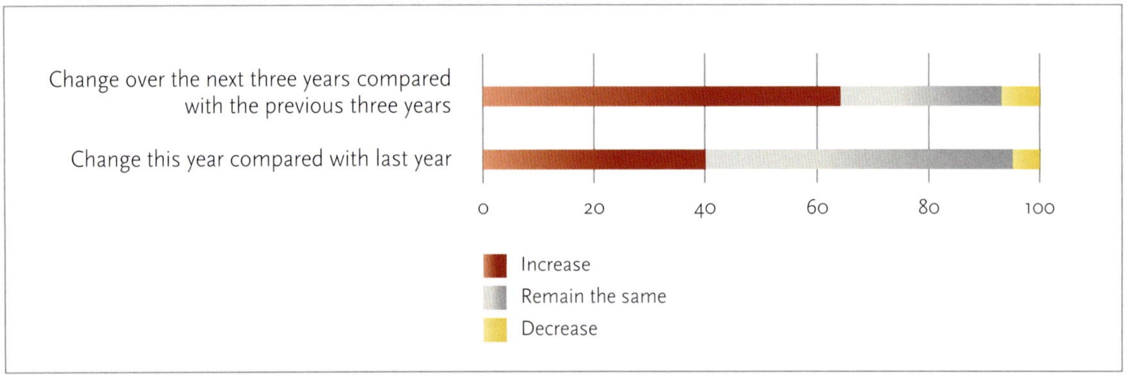

Question 3. What is the main constraint to cross-border investment in the next 12 months and the next three years?

Percent of respondents

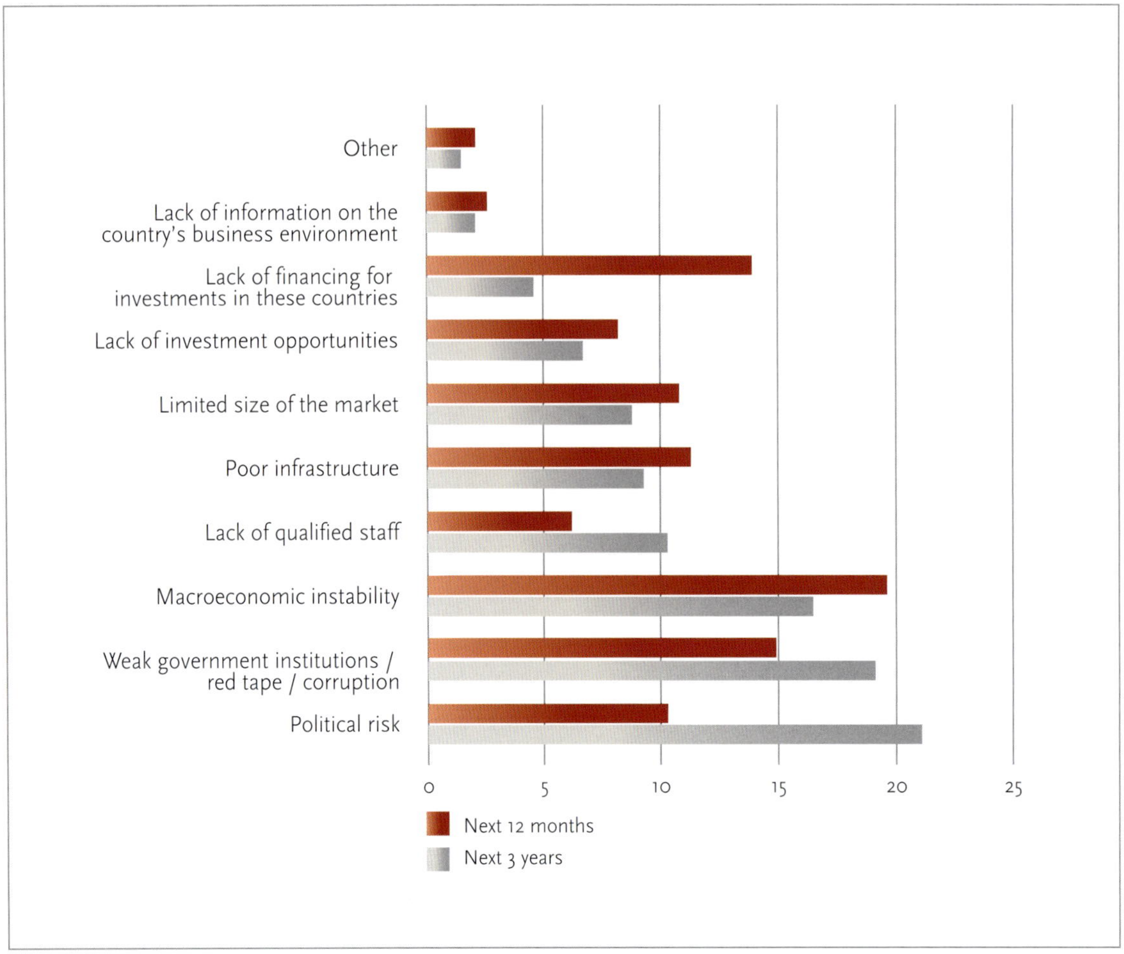

QUESTION 4. DOES YOUR COMPANY INVEST OR PLAN TO INVEST IN ANY OF THE FOLLOWING COUNTRIES?

Percent of respondents

	Currently invest	Plan to invest within the next three years	Total
Afghanistan	7	9	16
Angola	9	7	16
Bosnia and Herzegovia	10	11	21
Burundi	2	4	6
Cameroon	6	7	13
Central African Republic	4	9	13
Chad	2	5	7
Comoros	2	4	6
Congo, Dem. Rep. of	8	8	16
Congo, Rep. of	4	6	10
Côte d'Ivoire	6	7	13
Djibouti	1	6	7
Eritrea	2	4	6
Equatorial Guinea	3	5	8
Gambia, The	2	5	7
Georgia	7	14	21
Guinea	3	5	8
Guinea-Bissau	4	3	7
Haiti	4	8	12
Iran, Islamic Rep.	6	10	16
Iraq	8	18	26
Kiribati	1	3	4
Kosovo	4	8	12
Liberia	2	5	7
Myanmar	2	5	7
Nepal	4	5	9
Nigeria	18	14	32
Papua New Guinea	7	6	13
Pakistan	17	10	27
São Tomé and Principe	4	5	9
Sierra Leone	2	3	5
Solomon Islands	1	4	5
Somalia	1	3	4
Sudan	3	5	8
Tajikistan	4	5	9
Timor-Leste	6	3	9
Togo	4	2	6
Tonga	1	3	4
Uzbekistan	8	8	16
Yemen, Rep.	1	3	4
West Bank and Gaza	1	4	5
Western Sahara	4	5	9
Zimbabwe	7	6	13

Question 5. Which of the following factors will pose the greatest constraint on investments by your company in the countries listed in the prior question?

Percent of respondents

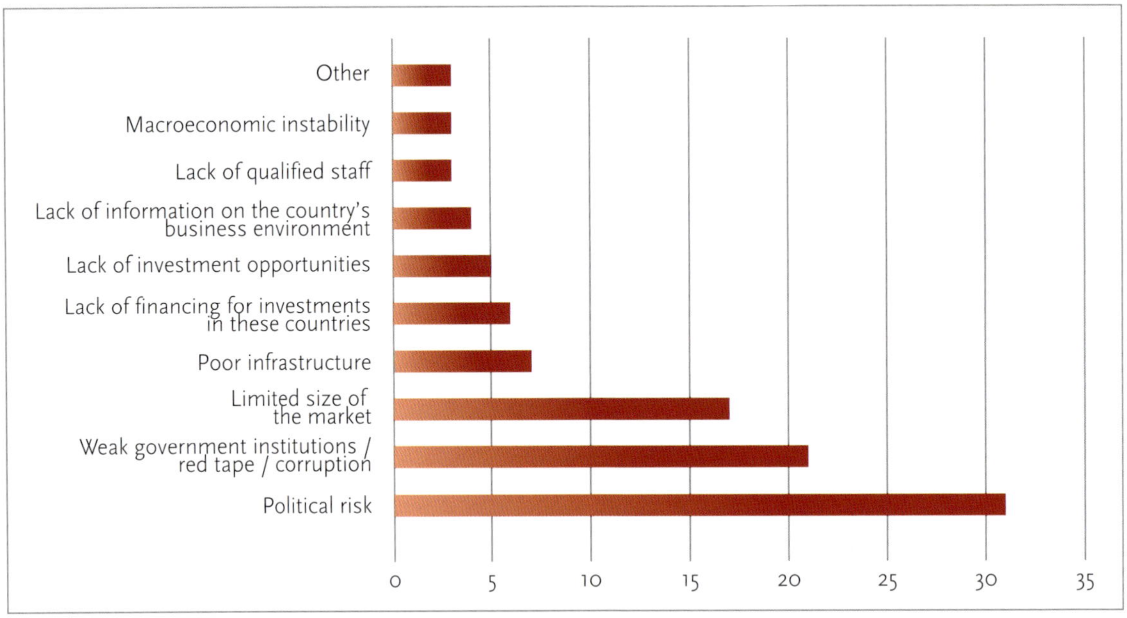

Question 6. What types of political risk are of most concern to your firm when investing in developing countries? Select up to three risks for each time frame.

Percent of respondents

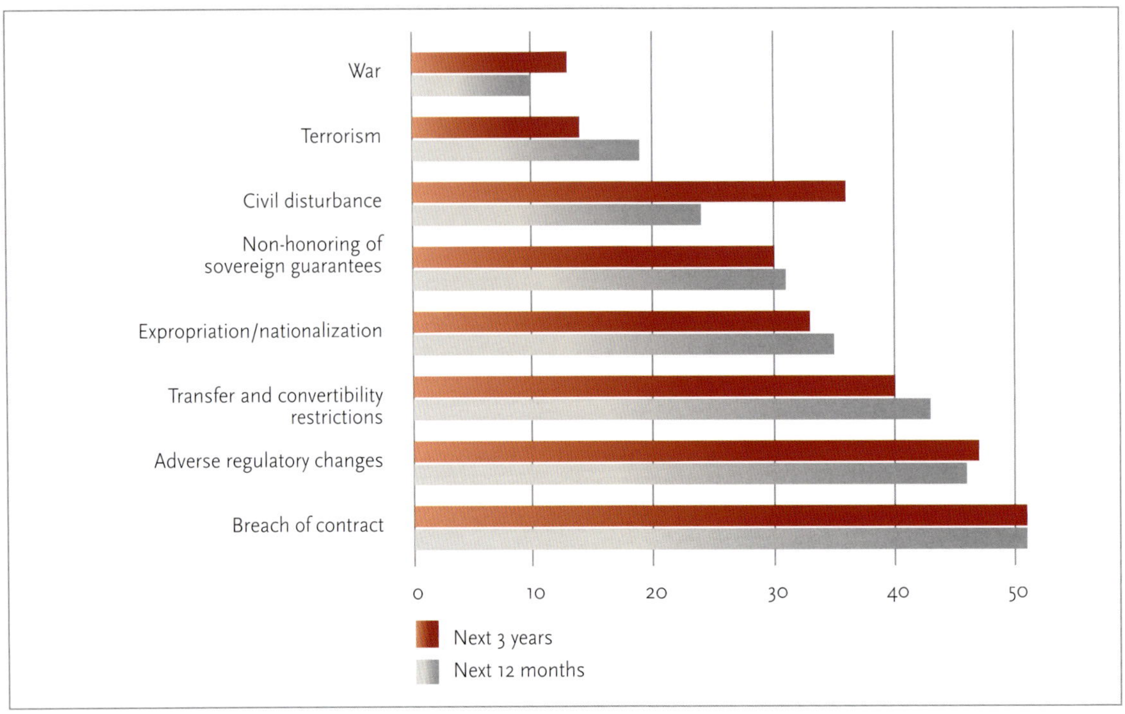

Question 7. How much importance does your firm assign to each of the risks listed below when deciding on the location of its foreign projects?

Percent of respondents

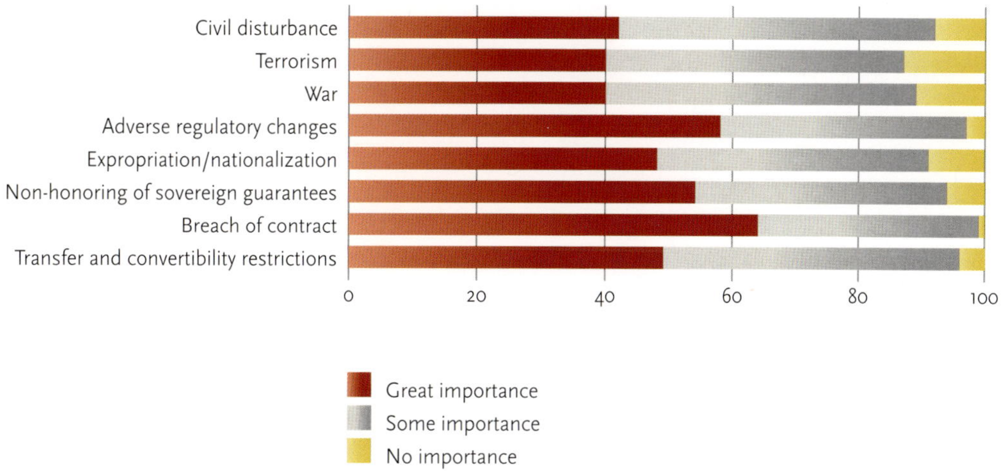

Question 8. In the developing countries where your firm invests presently, what is the perceived level for each of the following risks?

Percent of respondents

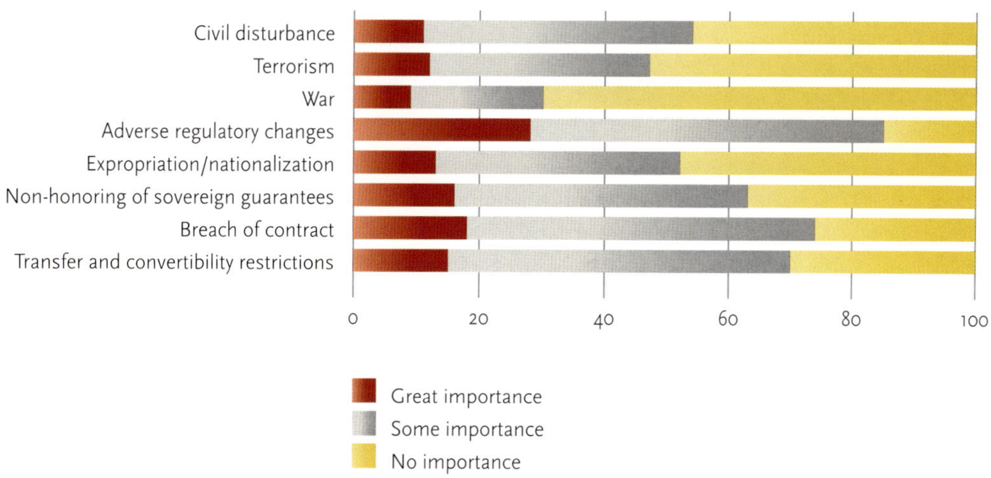

Question 9. In the developing countries where your firm invests presently, how do each of the risks listed below affect your company?

Percent of respondents

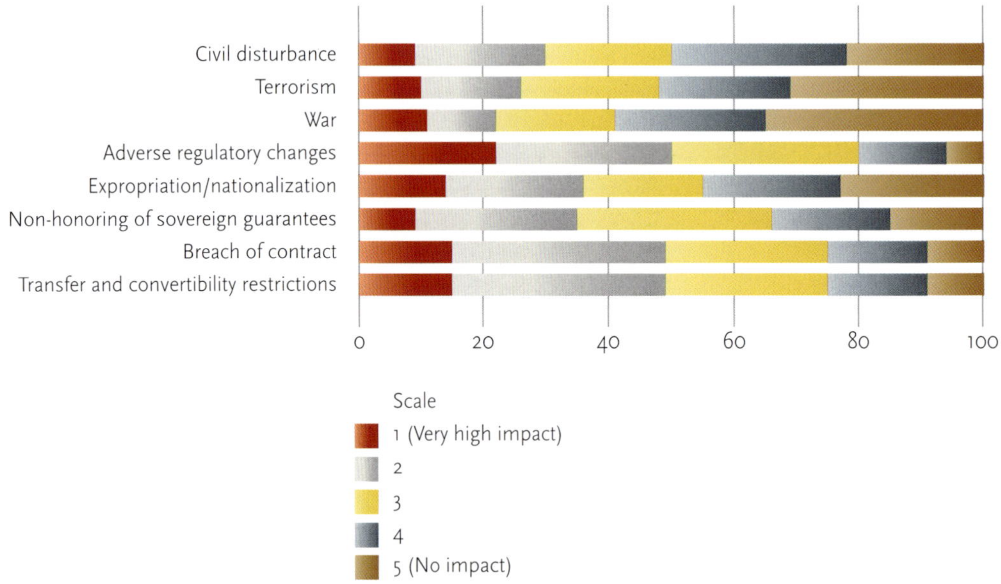

Question 10. In the past three years, has your company experienced financial losses caused by any of the following risks? Select all that apply.

Percent of respondents

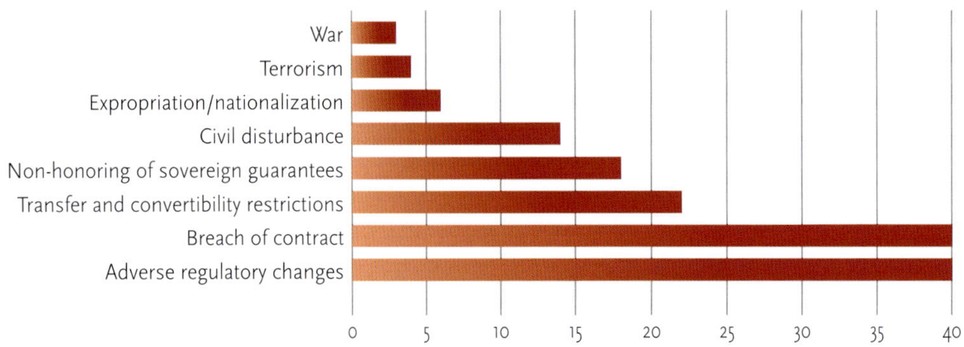

QUESTION 11. TO YOUR KNOWLEDGE, HAVE ANY OF THE FOLLOWING RISKS CAUSED YOUR COMPANY TO WITHDRAW AN EXISTING INVESTMENT OR CANCEL PLANNED INVESTMENTS OVER THE PAST 12 MONTHS?

Percent of respondents

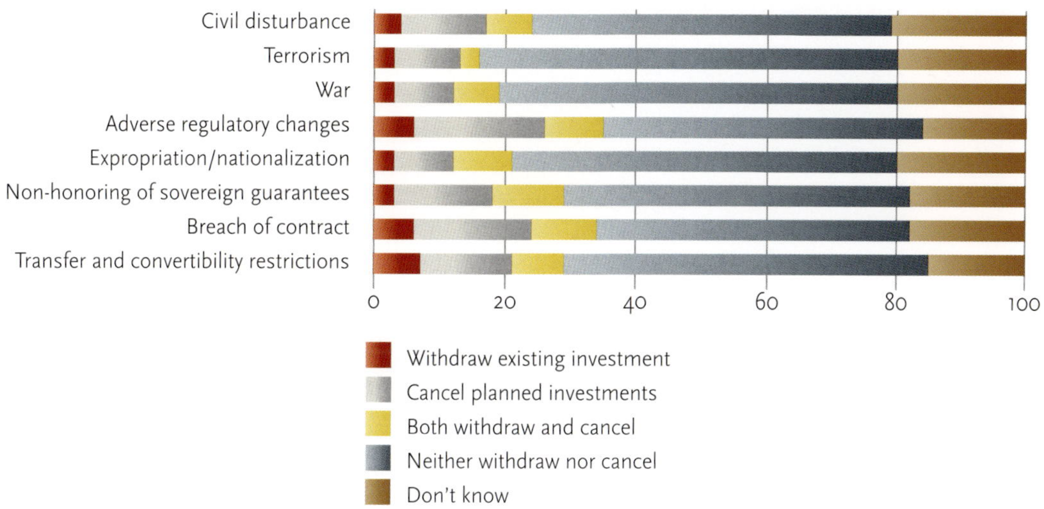

Question 12. What tools/mechanisms does your company use to mitigate political risk when investing in developing countries? Select all that apply.

Percent of respondents

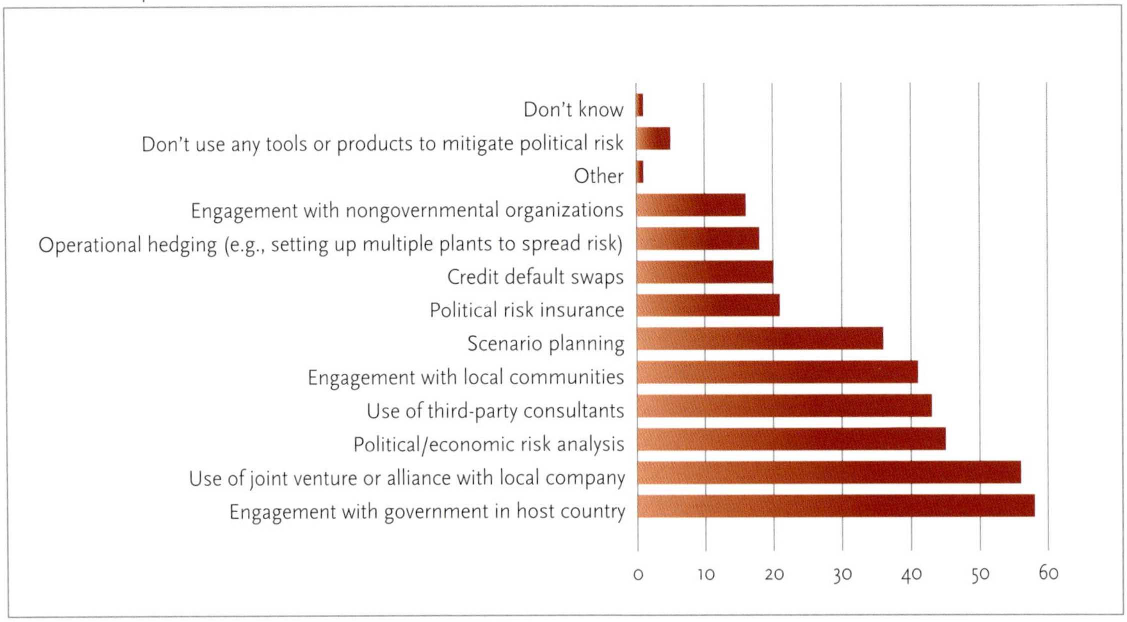

Question 13. In your opinion, in the countries where your company invests, what are the most effective tools or mechanisms available to your firm for alleviating each of the following risks? Select one tool for each risk.

Percent of respondents

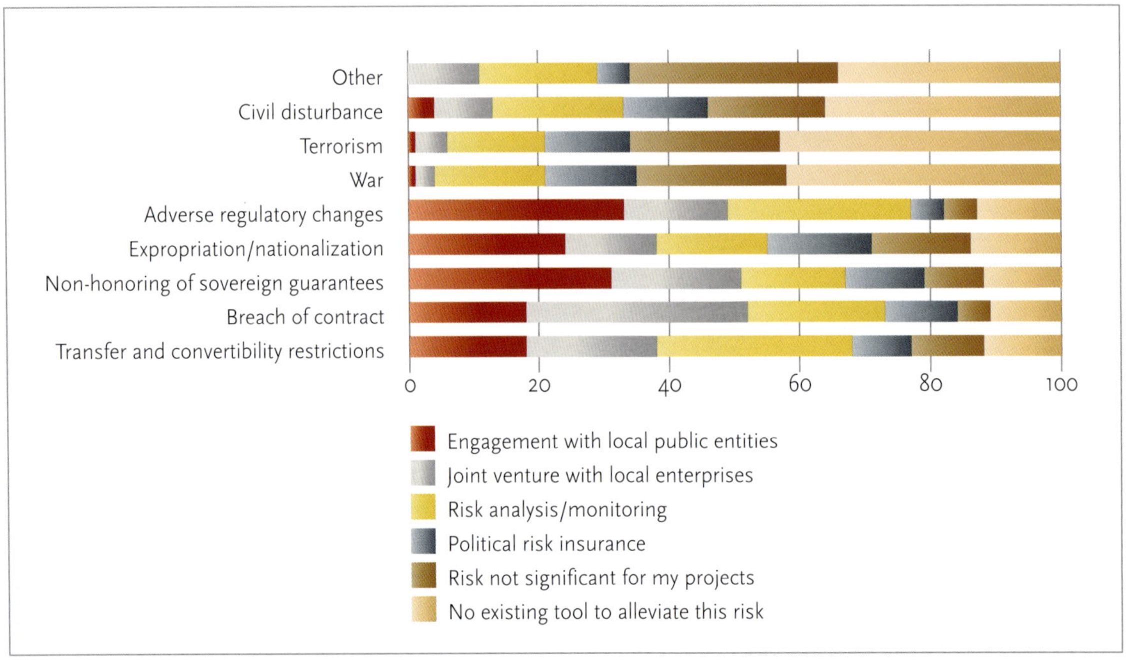

Appendix 3 Countries[a] Rated in the Two Highest Political Violence[b] Risk Categories by the Political Risk Insurance Industry on January 1, 2010

Countries

Afghanistan
Angola
Bosnia and Herzegovina
Burundi
Cameroon
Central African Republic
Chad
Comoros
Congo, Dem. Rep. of
Congo, Rep. of
Côte d'Ivoire
Djibouti
Equatorial Guinea
Eritrea
Gambia, The
Georgia
Guinea
Guinea-Bissau
Haiti
Iran, Islamic Rep. of
Iraq
Kiribati
Kosovo
Liberia
Myanmar
Nepal
Nigeria
Pakistan
Papua New Guinea
Saõ Tomé and Principe
Sierra Leone
Solomon Islands
Somalia
Sudan
Tajikistan
Timor-Leste
Togo
Tonga
Uzbekistan
Yemen, Rep. of
Zimbabwe

Territories

West Bank and Gaza
Western Sahara

[a] This list was used in the analysis presented in this report.

[b] War, civil disturbance, and terrorism.

Appendix 4 Number of BITs Concluded as of June 2010 by Countries or Territories Rated in the Two Highest Political Violence Risk Categories

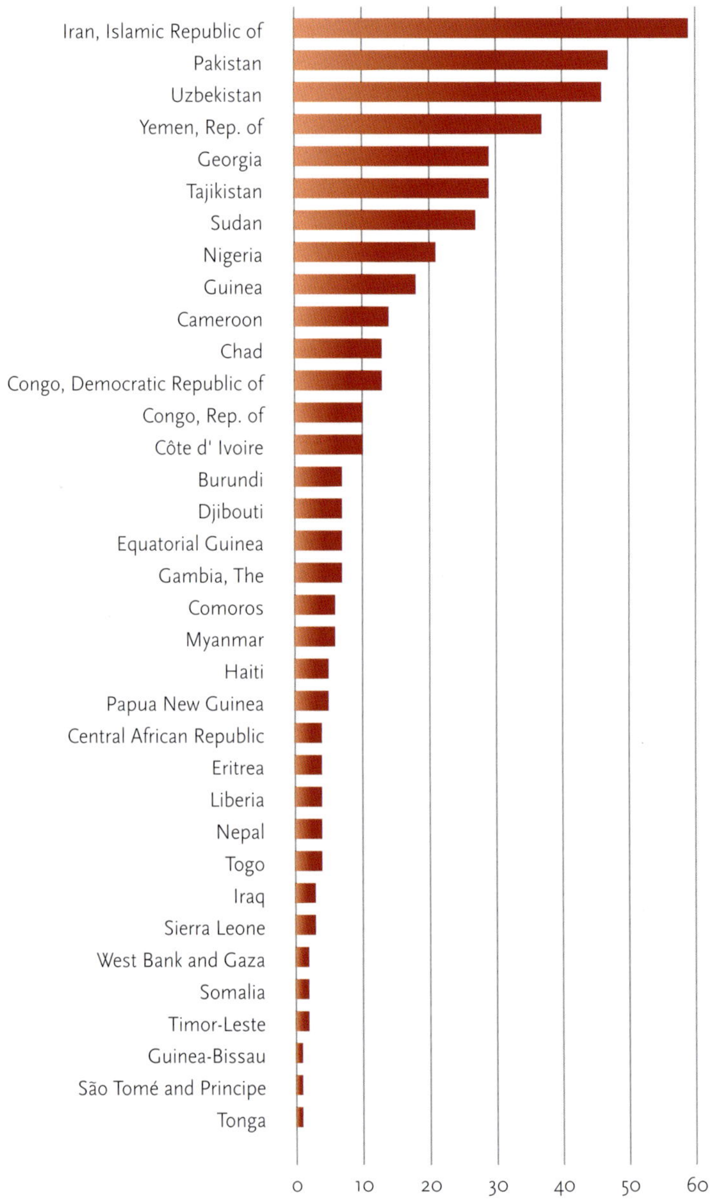

Source: UNCTAD database on International Investment Agreements.

Appendix 5 Conflict and Foreign Direct Investment: A Review of the Academic Literature

Conflict generally exerts a negative influence on foreign direct investment (FDI). According to the Multilateral Investment Guarantee Agency's (MIGA) own findings (see appendix 7), the outbreak of conflict results in fewer greenfield FDI projects and smaller investment values, compared to nonconflict countries. Other studies confirm that political instability in general—which incorporates conflict—has a negative effect on the volume of FDI, while some suggest that political stability increases the likelihood of a country being selected as an investment location.[1] Other research finds no evidence that political instability (constructed as an index that includes social unrest, conflict, violence, and terrorism) influences the probability of a country being selected as a destination for FDI, though there is evidence that political instability reduces investment value.[2]

Most foreign investors attempt to assess what the probability of conflict is and how it will affect expected rates of return before they decide to invest. If anticipated, conflict may not change the behavior of foreign direct investors.[3] Conflict cannot always be foreseen, however, and the risk of unexpected political violence also factors into investors' decision of where to invest, thus potentially leading to a scaling down and cancelation of investment plans.

The nature of conflict also matters. Civil war has been found to have the worst impact on FDI, compared to interstate war or terrorism. Interstate war, when anticipated, does not appear to affect the probability of a country being selected as an investment destination, nor the amount of FDI it receives.[4] Similarly, terrorism—whether anticipated or not—does not seem to influence investors' choices of investment destinations. Unanticipated civil war, conversely, will lower the probability of a country being chosen as an investment destination and will have a negative effect on FDI flows.

Once investments have been made, whether the conflict results in divestment from existing projects largely depends on industry and project characteristics.[5] Investments that either require high sunk costs or a long-term horizon, such as those in natural resource extraction, or that cannot be relocated, such as agriculture projects, are more likely to be maintained. However, relocation is more likely in industries that not only are more labor than capital intensive, but also rely on exports rather than local markets, such as textile and apparel manufacturing. Firms that are part of international supply chains are also good candidates for relocation, because the disruption of the local production process has international implications. The likelihood of relocation also increases in industries that make extensive use of intangible assets. Yet, how long an investor has been operating in the country may also influence the decision to stay or divest, regardless of the industry.

Once political violence abates, FDI, if well managed, can contribute to economic development, which reduces the risk that conflict may resurface. One study[6] estimates that the risk of conflict recurrence falls to 27 percent in economies that grow by 10 percent in the decade following the end of conflict. (That risk increases to 42 percent in economies that are stagnant.) FDI can also help integrate CAF countries into international production networks, a move that has been found to reduce bilateral military conflict.[7] A high ratio of FDI stock to GDP has also been associated with lower conflict in poor countries, thanks to the increase in available resources and opportunities.[8] Finally, FDI has been found to indirectly reduce terrorist incidents by promoting economic development in host countries.[9]

[1] Margit Bussmann, 2010, "Foreign Direct Investment and Militarized International Conflict," *Journal of Peace Research*, 47: 143–53; Quan Li, 2006, "Political Violence and Foreign Direct Investment," in *Research in Global Strategic Management, Regional Economic Integration*, Michele Fratianni and Alan M. Rugman, eds., 225–49, Oxford: Elsevier Ltd.; Douglas Nigh, 1985, "The Effect of Political Events on United States Direct Foreign Investment: A Pooled Time-Series Cross-Sectional Analysis," *Journal of International Business Studies*, 16: 1–17; Friedrich Schneider and Bruno S. Frey, 1985, "Economic and Political Determinants of Foreign Direct Investment," *World Development*, 13: 161–75; Douglas Woodward and Robert Rolfe, 1993, "The Location of Export-Oriented Foreign Direct Investment in the Caribbean Basin," *Journal of International Business Studies*, 24: 121–44.

2 Steven Globerman and Daniel Shapiro, 2003, "Governance Infrastructure and US Foreign Direct Investment," *Journal of International Business Studies*, 34: 315–26.

3 Quan Li, 2008, "Foreign Direct Investment and Interstate Military Conflict," *Journal of International Affairs*, 62: 53–66.

4 Quan Li, 2006, "Political Violence and Foreign Direct Investment," in *Research in Global Strategic Management, Regional Economic Integration*, Michele Fratianni and Alan M. Rugman, eds., 225–49. Oxford: Elsevier Ltd. For an analysis of how different types of conflict affect FDI, see also Yi-hung Chiou, 2010, "Investing for Peace? Foreign Direct Investment and Conflict Initiation," paper presented at the annual meeting of the Midwest Political Science Association 67th Annual National Conference, Chicago, IL.

5 Andreea S. Mihalache, 2010, "Firm Characteristics and Perceptions of Threat from Political Violence," Pennsylvania State University, unpublished; Andreea S. Micalache, 2009, "Who's Afraid of Political Violence? Evidence from Industry Level FDI flows," unpublished.

6 Paul Collier, Anke Hoeffler and Måns Soderböm, 2008, "Post-Conflict Risks." *Journal of Peace Research*, 45: 461–78.

7 Erik Gartzke, Quan Li, and Charles Boehmer, 2001, "Investing in the Peace: Economic Interdependence and International Conflict," *International Organization*, 55: 391–438; Eric Gartzke and Quan Li, 2003, "The Shadow of the Invisible Hand: War, Peace, and Economic Globalization," *International Studies Quarterly*, 47: 561–86.

8 John Rothgeb, 1990, "Investment Dependence and Political Conflict in Third World Countries," *Journal of Peace Research*, 27: 255–72.

9 Quan Li and Drew Schaub, 2004, "Economic Globalization and Transnational Terrorist Incidents: A Pooled Time Series Analysis," *Journal of Conflict Resolution*, 48: 230–58.

APPENDIX 6 MIGA-EIU CAF INVESTORS SURVEY

This appendix is based on a survey that is of 60 multinational enterprises (MNE) with investments in at least one conflict-affected and fragile (CAF) state and that was conducted on the Multilateral Investment Guarantee Agency's (MIGA) behalf by the Economist Intelligence Unit (EIU) in July 2010 through telephone interviews. The survey intended to capture (i) respondents' views on political risk in CAF states, (ii) investment plans in these countries going forward, (iii) importance of political risk as a deterrent to investment, (iv) experience with losses caused by political risk events, and (v) the extent to which the availability of political risk insurance for these countries would help to facilitate cross-border investments. The data provided next present the responses of senior executives from these companies.

FIGURE A6.1 WHAT IS YOUR INDUSTRY SECTOR?

Percent of respondents

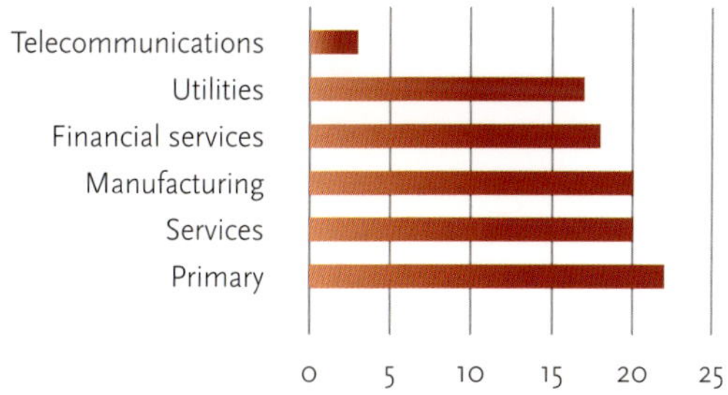

FIGURE A6.2 WHAT IS YOUR COMPANY'S GLOBAL ANNUAL REVENUE?

Percent of respondents

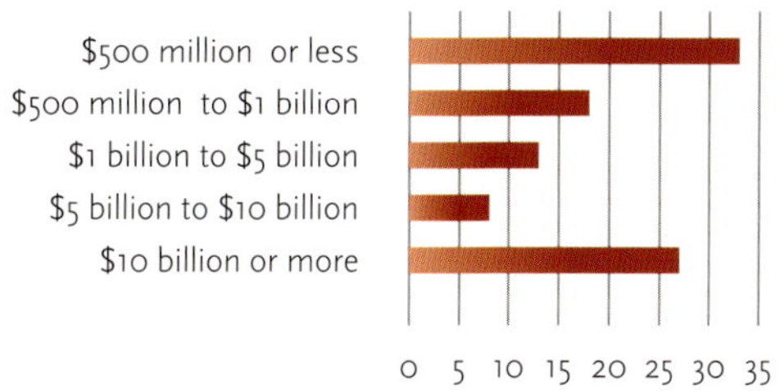

FIGURE A6.3 IN WHICH COUNTRY IS YOUR COMPANY'S HEADQUARTERS?
Percent of respondents

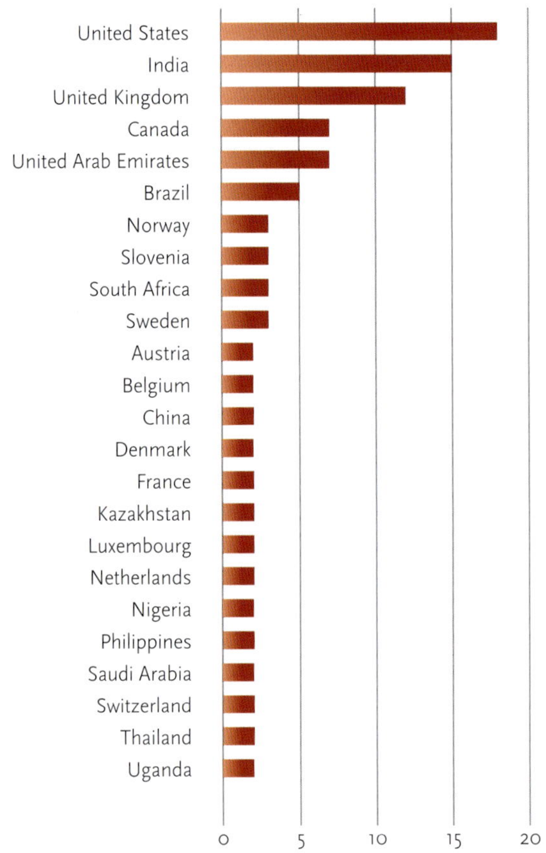

Question 1. Do you have an existing investment or plan to invest within the next three years in the following countries? Select up to five, and please choose the most important in terms of investment amount.

Percent of respondents

	Currently invest	Plan to invest in next three years
Afghanistan	2	3
Angola	10	12
Bosnia and Herzegovina	13	13
Burundi	2	3
Cameroon	7	7
Central African Republic	2	3
Comoros	0	2
Congo, Dem. Rep. of	8	8
Congo, Rep.	2	3
Côte d'Ivoire	5	3
Gambia, The	2	0
Georgia	15	10
Guinea	2	2
Haiti	3	3
Iran, Islamic Rep. of	0	3
Iraq	2	2
Myanmar	7	5
Nepal	3	3
Nigeria	3	3
Papua New Guinea	2	2
Pakistan	2	2
Sierra Leone	2	2
Sudan	8	7
Tajikistan	5	3
Timor-Leste	0	2
Yemen, Rep. of	8	7
Zimbabwe	7	7

Question 2. How do you expect your company's investment in the following countries to change over the next 12 months compared with the past 12 months?

Percent of respondents

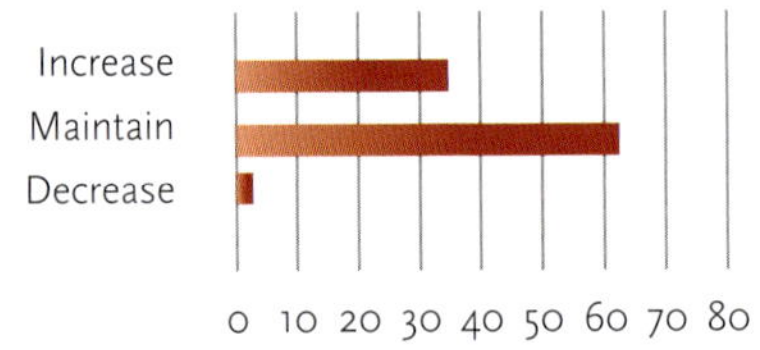

Question 3. In your opinion, what are the main constraining factors for further investment in these countries? Select the top three for each country and rank them, where 1 is your top choice.

Percent of responses

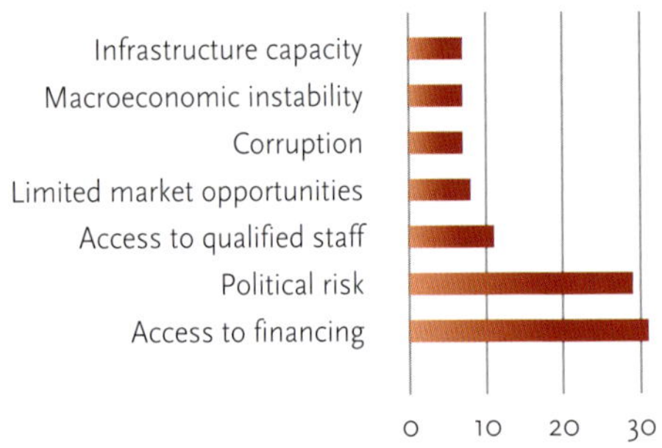

Question 4. In your opinion, what types of political risk are of most concern in these countries? Select the top three for each country and rank them, where 1 is your top choice.

Percent of respondents

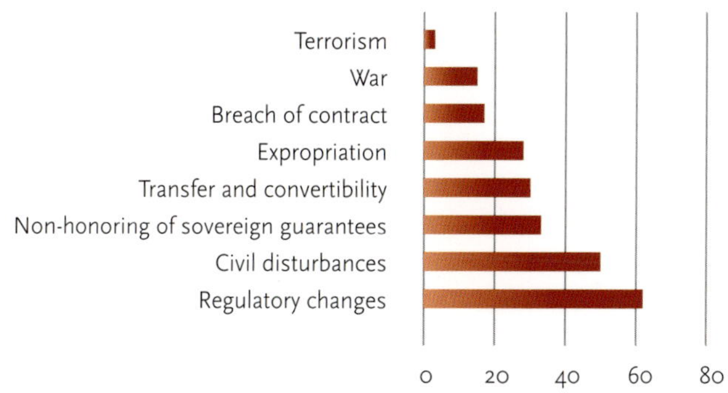

Question 5. Has your company experienced any financial losses caused by these political risks in the past? Select all that apply for each country or territory.

Percent of respondents

Question 6. In the past 12 months has your company scaled back, canceled or delayed investment in these countries because of political risk? Select all that apply for each country or territory?

Percent of respondents

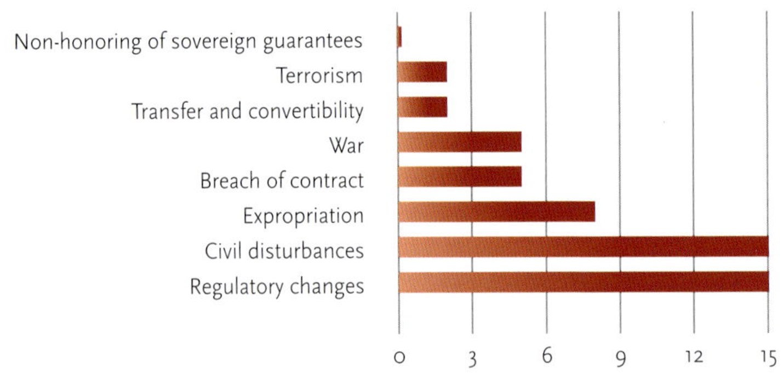

Question 7. How does your company mitigate these risks? Select all that apply for each country or territory.

Percent of responses

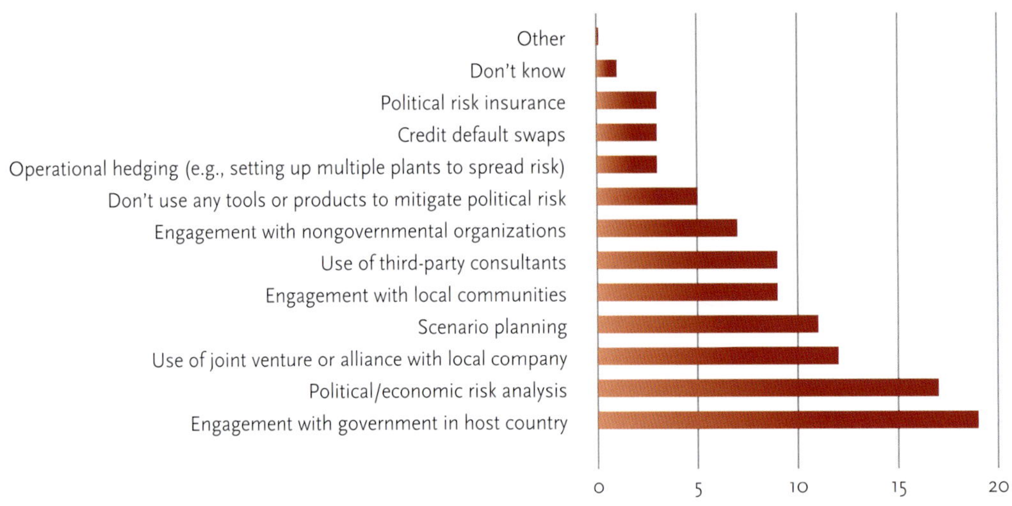

Question 8. Have you sought coverage of these risks through political risk insurance?

Percent of respondents

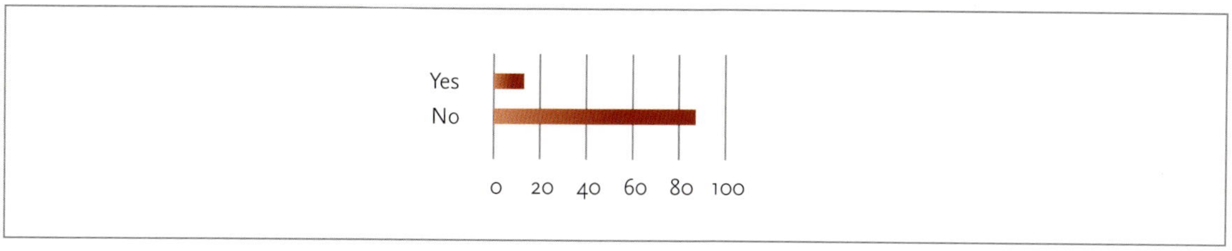

Question 9. If you use political risk insurance for investment in these countries, why do you use it? Select all that apply.

Percent of respondents

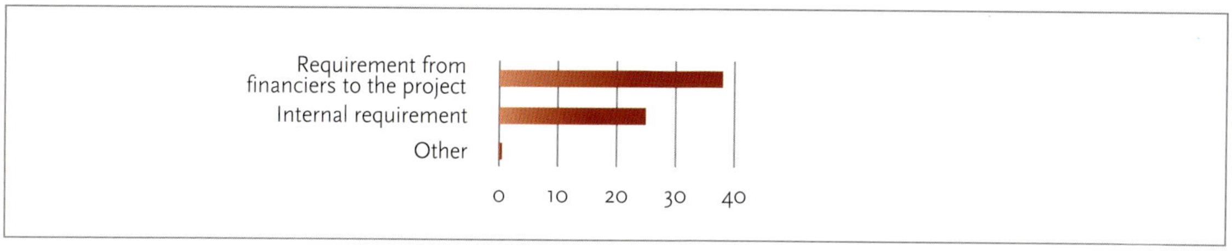

Question 10. What are your primary reasons for not using political risk insurance in these selected countries? Select all that apply.

Percent of respondents

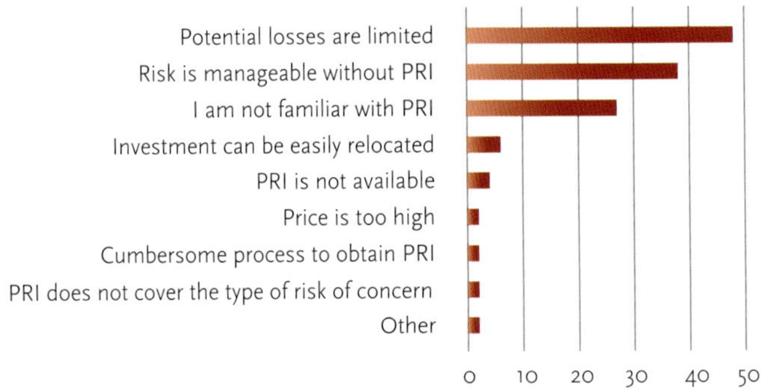

Question 11. Why is political risk not a deterrent for investment in these countries? Select all that apply.

Percent of responses

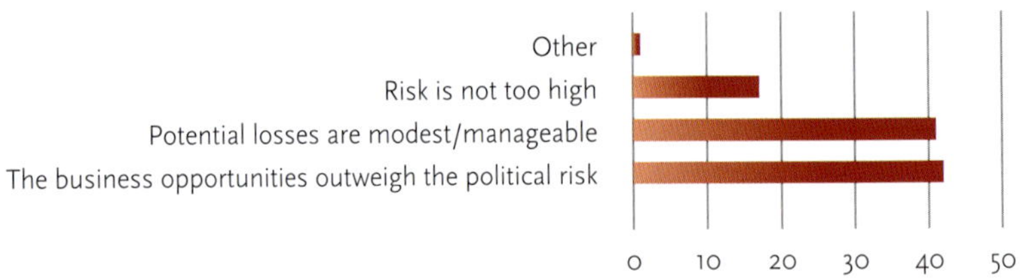

Appendix 7 Model Specification, Methodology, and Regression Results

This appendix describes the model specification, data sources, and regression results of the analysis presented in chapter 2. A more detailed description can be found in Raphael Reinke, 2010, "Who Bites the Bullet? A Sectoral Analysis of FDI in Conflict-Affected Countries," Tubingen: Eberhald-Karls University, master's thesis.

Model Specification and Data Sources

The dependent variable in this analysis is the number of investment projects per industry, country, and year. Greenfield cross-border investment data (number of projects and value) are from fDI Markets, a *Financial Times* database covering an estimated 80 percent of cross-border greenfield investments worldwide across 23 sectors. The sample used in this analysis comprises all greenfield investment projects in developing countries (defined as those that were not members of OECD before 1994) for the period 2003–2009.

The independent variable is a dummy variable indicating the existence of conflict. Fragile countries that are not currently in a conflict were excluded from the analysis. The binary conflict variable was based on a classification used by the Department of Peace and Conflict Research in Uppsala and by the Peace Research Institute in Oslo (PRIO), which identifies a conflict episode when 25 deaths are reached per year in countries experiencing conflict and a cumulative death toll of at least 1,000 for the entire conflict.

In addition, several control variables were included: GDP per capita and population size (controlling for market size), GDP per capita growth (controlling for market growth), and fixed/mobile subscriptions (controlling for infrastructure quality). The control variable data are from the World Bank and the Economist Intelligence Unit.

Because the dependent variable is a count variable and because of the dispersion pattern of the data, the model was specified as a negative binomial regression. To measure the statistical impact of conflict on the number of projects and value of investments, the analysis followed three approaches: (i) a country panel analysis, (ii) an industry panel analysis, and (iii) a cross-sectional industry analysis.

Country Panel Analysis

The estimation made at the country level seeks to assess the overall impact of conflict on investment decisions; therefore, data are aggregated from individual investment decisions to the country level. The data are then presented in the form of a country-year panel. In the first analysis the expected value of the number of investment projects in a particular country is denoted by μ^{NFDI}. X_1 to X_m represent the control variables, and D_{confl} is the conflict dummy variable. The resulting econometric model is the following:

$$\log(\mu^{NFDI}_{j,t}) = \beta_o + \beta_1 X_{1,,j,t-1} + \ldots + \beta_m X_{m,j,t-1} + \beta_{confl} D_{confl,,j,t-1} + \nu_j + \epsilon_{j,t}$$

with $_j$ indicating the country and $_t$ the year. The country-specific effect is included in the equation as ν_j, and the error term is the final $\epsilon_{j,t}$.

Given the time lag between investment decisions and actual investments (because financing, among other things, needs to be arranged), all contingent variables in the equation include a one-year time lag, which is represented by the index $_{t-1}$. All of the regressions, therefore, are presented with this time lag.

The second analysis at country level complements the one based on the number of investment projects by examining the individual projects' investment value by country. Although there may be some sector bias when one looks at investment values (resulting from industry-specific investment estimation assumptions), this bias should disappear when aggregated at the country level. The industry mix within each specific country may still remain an issue, however.

The model is a log regression that takes into account the fact that investment values are highly skewed. The estimation equation is the following:

$$\log(VFDI_{,t}) = \beta o + \beta_1 X_{1,,j,t-1} + \ldots + \beta_m X_{m,j,t-1} + \beta_{confl} D_{confl,,j,t-1} + \nu_j + \epsilon_{j,t}$$

where VFDI is the value of cross-border greenfield investment in a country across all sectors.

Industry (Sector) Panel Analysis

Analyzing the impact that industry characteristics have on investment decisions poses a problem to the models shown above because including an industry specification increases the dimension of the panel. As a result, each industry is analyzed in (i) a separate country-year panel, and (ii) a cross-sectional analysis, where the dependent variable is the annual average for the period 2003–2009, thus essentially collapsing the time dimension.

Because the industry panel includes only investments in each industry (and not all that occur in that country-year panel), the equation is the following:

$$\log(\mu^{NFDI(i)}_{j,t}) = \beta_o + \beta_1 X_{1,,j,t-1} + \ldots + \beta_m X_{m,j,t-1} + \beta_{confl} D_{confl,,j,t-1} + \nu_j + \epsilon_{j,t}$$

where NFDI(i) represents the number of investment projects in sector i and μNFDI(i) stands for the expected number of investment projects in sector i. The equation is then estimated for each sector (industry), and coefficients are compared across various sectors to test whether conflict influences foreign investor behavior more markedly in one sector than another.

The advantages of this method are capturing the time dimension (thus permitting the analysis of conflict and postconflict effects in a given industry and country) and highlighting sectoral differences in response to conflict. It also has disadvantages: serial correlation could cause underestimated standard errors, thus weakening the explanatory power of the model. Most important, conflict coefficients were found statistically significant in only four industries (see the regression tables that follow).

Cross-Sectional Analysis

The second approach to analyze sector-specific impacts is to collapse the time dimension and to use annual averages. Again, separate regressions were run for each sector using the following equation:

$$\log(\mu^{NFDI(i)}_{j}) = \beta_o + \beta 1\, X1_{,,j} + \ldots + \beta_m X_{m,j} + \beta_{confl} D_{confl,,j,} + \nu_j + \epsilon_{j,t}$$

As in the panel model mentioned earlier, the equation is estimated separately for each sector. Thus, the estimated coefficients and the standard errors permit us to understand the impact that conflict has on investment decisions in a particular sector.

Table A7.1 Regression Results

Country Panel Analysis: Projects

Dependent variable: Number of projects

Independent variable	Model 1	Model 2
Population	0.0018***	0.0018***
	(0.0003)	(0.0003)
GDP per capita	0.0864***	0.0838***
	(0.0204)	(0.0206)
GDP per capital growth	-0.0039	-0.0029
	(0.0050)	(0.0051)
Fixed-line telephone	0.0154***	0.0137***
	(0.0055)	(0.0056)
Conflict dummy	-0.4108**	-0.5885***
	(0.1793)	(0.2061)
Postconflict dummy	–	-0.3048*
	–	(0.1688)
Constant	1.3029***	1.3645***
	(0.1259)	(0.1297)
Number of observations	877	877
Number of groups	151	151
Log-likelihood	-2,031.34	-2,029.61

*Note: GDP=gross domestic product; *** $p < 0.01$, ** $p < 0.05$, * $p < 0.1$; standard errors in parentheses.*
Model: Fixed effects for negative binomial regression.

TABLE A7.2 REGRESSION RESULTS

Country Panel Analysis: Investment

Dependent variable: Total value of investment

Independent variable	Model 1	Model 2
Population	0.0168*	0.0144
	(0.0102)	(0.0088)
GDP per capita	0.1500**	0.1486**
	(0.0746)	(0.0745)
GDP per capital growth	0.0083	0.0080
	(0.0131)	(0.0131)
Fixed-line telephone	0.0350**	0.0299*
	(0.0161)	(0.0178)
Conflict dummy	-1.7381***	-2.2850***
	(0.5667)	(0.7058)
Postconflict dummy	–	-0.6069
		(0.4701)
Constant	19.0200***	19.2707***
	(0.5748)	(0.5253)
Number of observations	748	748
R^2 within	0.0516	0.0588
R^2 between	0.1721	0.1611
R^2 overall	0.1738	0.1707

*Note: GDP=gross domestic product; *** p < 0.01, ** p < 0.05, * p < 0.1; standard errors in parentheses.*
Model: Fixed effects estimation with robust standard errors clustered by country.

Table A7.3 Regression Results

Industry (Sector) Panel Analysis: Projects

Dependent Variable: Number of projects

	Energy	Automobiles and components	Capital goods	Consumer services	Communications	Consumer durables	Consumer staples	Financial services
Population	0.0014*	0.0008	0.0016***	0.0016**	0.0015***	0.0004	0.0014**	0.0023***
	(0.0007)	(0.0005)	(0.0005)	(0.0006)	(0.0006)	(0.0006)	(0.0006)	(0.0005)
GDP per capita	-0.0032	-0.0134	0.0428	0.0585	0.1512***	0.0023	-0.0157	0.0133
	(0.0588)	(0.0403)	(0.0305)	(0.0430)	(0.0529)	(0.0582)	(0.0489)	(0.0346)
GDP growth	0.0153	-0.0048	-0.0050	-0.0060	-0.0109	0.0011	-0.0149	0.0226**
	(0.0116)	(0.0151)	(0.0098)	(0.0097)	(0.0109)	(0.0224)	(0.0158)	(0.0111)
Phone sub-scriptions	0.0104***	0.0015	0.0084***	0.0131***	0.0011	0.0009	0.0048***	0.0086***
	(0.0016)	(0.0015)	(0.0013)	(0.0014)	(0.0017)	(0.0020)	(0.0015)	(0.0012)
Conflict dummy	-0.2366	-0.7413*	-0.7232*	0.0956	-0.3970	-0.4924	-0.3464	- 0.2168
	(0.3224)	(0.3827)	(0.3706)	(0.3553)	(0.3552)	(0.5111)	(0.3811)	(0.2855)
Constant	0.4870*	1.8756***	0.9368***	0.9605***	1.0072***	1.6505***	1.2965***	0.4193**
	(0.2467)	(0.3528)	(0.2736)	(0.3577)	(0.2911)	(0.4159)	(0.3647)	(0.1954)
Number of observations	699	483	590	639	687	469	624	754
Number of groups	120	82	101	110	118	79	106	131
Log-likelihood	-850.18	-616.78	-749.04	-739.06	-704.19	-466.05	-678.59	-1,007.55

*Note: GDP=gross domestic product; *** $p < 0.01$, ** $p < 0.05$, * $p < 0.1$; standard errors in parentheses.*
Model: Fixed effects for negative binomial regression.

Table A7.3 Regression Results (cont'd)

Industry (Sector) Panel Analysis: Projects

Dependent variable: Number of projects

	Health care	Hotels, restaurants, and leisure	Materials	Metals and mining	Real estate	Software and IT services	Technology hardware	Transportation
Population	0.0035	0.0008	0.0002	0.0007	0.0029**	0.0008*	0.0001	0.0010*
	(0.0022)	(0.0005)	(0.0005)	(0.0006)	(0.0012)	(0.0005)	(0.0005)	(0.0006)
GDP per capita	0.0239	0.0202	-0.0405	0.0656	0.0323	0.0557**	0.0329	0.0689
	(0.0407)	(0.0325)	(0.0311)	(0.0683)	(0.0415)	(0.0255)	(0.0301)	(0.0621)
GDP growth	-0.0496***	0.0104	0.0234**	0.0043	0.0470***	0.0181	0.0153	-0.0122
	(0.0156)	(0.0156)	(0.0118)	(0.0150)	(0.0178)	(0.0128)	(0.0165)	(0.0141)
Phone subscriptions	0.0054***	0.068***	0.0025**	0.0004	0.0142***	0.0052***	-0.0068***	0.0025*
	(0.0018)	(0.0015)	(0.0011)	(0.0016)	(0.0018)	(0.0013)	(0.0018)	(0.0015)
Conflict dummy	-1.3077*	0.0472	-0.1855	0.3141	-0.3076	-0.0702	-1.0812*	-0.1058
	(0.7236)	(0.4340)	(0.3758)	(0.3826)	(0.5086)	(0.3631)	(0.5561)	(0.3946)
Constant	2.1205***	0.4713	1.9715***	1.3777***	-1.2063***	1.1736***	2.2345***	1.7388***
	(0.6449)	(0.3038)	(0.3325)	(0.2952)	(0.2732)	(0.2838)	(0.4491)	(0.3866)
Number of observations	477	611	610	679	494	531	451	607
Number of groups	81	104	105	117	84	90	77	103
Log-likelihood	-464.23	-681.44	-805.83	-792.36	-592.82	-704.52	-514.03	-662.18

*Note: GDP=gross domestic product; *** $p < 0.01$, ** $p < 0.05$, * $p < 0.1$; standard errors in parentheses; IT=information technology.*
Model: Fixed effects for negative binomial regression.

TABLE A7.4 REGRESSION RESULTS

Cross-Sectional Analysis: Projects

Dependent variable: Number of projects

	Energy	Automobiles and components	Capital goods	Consumer services	Communications	Consumer durables	Consumer staples	Financial services
Population	0.0110	0.0329**	0.0142	0.0165*	0.0098	0.0116*	0.0158*	0.0073
	(0.0074)	(0.0137)	(0.0105)	(0.0098)	(0.0064)	(0.0065)	(0.0086)	(0.0060)
GDP per capita	0.0559*	- 0559	0.0304	0.1024***	0.0126	-.0646*	-.0559	0.0312
	(0.0317)	(0.0341)	(0.0394)	(0.0311)	(0.0288)	(0.0360)	(0.0356)	(0.0256)
GDP growth	0.1520***	0.3022***	0.1542*	0.1998***	0.0765	0.1950**	0.0501	0.1724***
	(0.0429)	(0.1057)	(0.0924)	(0.0556)	(0.0521)	(0.0838)	(0.0485)	(0.0468)
Fixed-line subscriptions	- .0083	0.1032***	0.0838***	0.0132	0.0077	0.0536***	0.0532***	0.0378***
	(0.0136)	(0.0211)	(0.0197)	(0.0164)	(0.0117)	(0.0178)	(0.0154)	(0.0115)
Conflict dummy	-.1468	-.4412**	-.0582***	-.1097***	-.0369	-.3387***	-.1674	-.0796
	(0.4115)	(0.6127)	(0.4015)	(0.3846)	(0.3398)	(0.4307)	(0.4173)	(0.1457)
Constant	5.5765***	0.6395	1.5356**	0.5024	3.5630***	1.0610*	2.4273***	2.6257***
	(0.3892)	(0.8527)	(0.6083)	(0.5753)	(0.3330)	(0.5830)	(0.4378)	(0.3354)
ln(alpha)	1.3387***	1.8432***	1.5109***	0.9961***	1.0688***	1.6044***	1.2320***	0.5956***
	(0.1238)	(0.1487)	(0.1157)	(0.1451)	(0.1220)	(0.1282)	(0.1284)	(0.1211)
Number of observations	152	152	152	152	152	152	152	152
Log-likelihood	-1,048.78	-616.11	-629.21	-488.31	-760.83	-462.87	-653.12	-786.77
Pseudo R^2	0.011	0.042	0.057	0.072	0.024	0.046	0.037	0.061

*Note: GDP=gross domestic product; *** $p < 0.01$, ** $p < 0.05$, * $p < 0.1$; standard errors in parentheses.*
Model: Negative binomial regression.
alpha: Over-dispersion parameter.

TABLE A7.4 REGRESSION RESULTS (CONT'D)

Cross-Sectional Analysis: Projects

Dependent variable: Number of projects

	Health care	Hotels, restaurants, and leisure	Materials	Metals and mining	Real estate	Software and IT services	Technology hardware	Transportation
Population	0.0104	0.0065	0.0118	0.0100	0.0138	0.0124	0.0243	0.0143**
	(0.0080)	(0.0058)	(0.0080)	(0.0066)	(0.0118)	(0.0099)	(0.0172)	(0.0067)
GDP per capita	0.0321	0.0909***	0.0575	- 0.0082	0.0499	0.0319	0.0695	0.0162
	(0.0385)	(0.0329)	(0.0370)	(0.0351)	(0.0378)	(0.0378)	(0.0673)	(0.0269)
GDP growth	0.0868	0.1327**	0.1079**	0.0127	0.1819	0.1048*	0.4052***	0.2482***
	(0.0792)	(0.0591)	(0.0444)	(0.0459)	(0.1120)	(0.0615)	(0.1353)	(0.0418)
Fixed-line subscriptions	0.0856***	0.0145	0.0362**	- 0.0111	0.0170	0.0801***	0.0716***	0.0355***
	(0.0187)	(0.0186)	(0.0170)	(0.0200)	(0.0224)	(0.0198)	(0.0249)	(0.0131)
Conflict dummy	-0.9180**	-1.5029***	-1.3464***	-0.9438***	-1.6072*	-0.8974**	-2.0862***	-0.8921***
	(0.3819)	(0.4219)	(0.3175)	(0.3177)	(0.9664)	(0.4443)	(0.7272)	(0.3299)
Constant	0.4425	3.5853***	3.7802***	5.6913***	4.5042***	0.8217	-0.2330	2.5257***
	(0.5895)	(0.44593)	(0.4254)	(0.3404)	(0.7724)	(0.5926)	(1.1769)	(0.4006)
ln(alpha)	1.4999***	1.4589***	1.5154***	1.3900***	2.1503***	1.3808***	2.0379***	1.3324***
	(0.1397)	(0.1228)	(0.1196)	(0.1193)	(0.1230)	(0.1273)	(0.1300)	(0.1321)
Number of observations	152	152	152	152	152	152	152	152
Log-likelihood	-460.58	-756.54	-809.00	-901.95	-751.86	-525.85	-475.63	-750.40
Pseudo R^2	0.068	0.029	0.028	0.016	0.009	0.066	0.056	0.047

*Note: GDP= gross domestic product; *** $p < 0.01$, ** $p < 0.05$, * $p < 0.1$; standard errors in parentheses; IT=infromation technology.*
Model: Negative binomial regression.
alpha: Over-dispersion parameter.

Appendix 8 Lloyd's Syndicates

Table A8.1 Lloyd's Syndicate Members

Company	
ACE Global Markets	Kiln
Amlin	Liberty Syn. Mgmt.
Ark	O'Farrell
Ascot	Marketform
Aspen	MAP
Beazley	Novae
Catlin	Starr PFR Consortium
Chaucer	Pembroke
Hardy	QBE
Hiscox	Talbot

Appendix 9 Berne Union and Prague Club Members

Table A9.1 Berne Union Members

Company	Country	Year joined
ASEI	Indonesia	1999
ASHRA	Israel	1958
CESCE	Spain	1972
ECGC	India	1957
ECGD	United Kingdom	1934
ECIC SA	South Africa	2004
EDC	Canada	1947
EFIC	Australia	1957
EGAP	Czech Republic	1996
EKF	Denmark	1997
EKN	Sweden	1947
EXIMBANKA SR	Slovak Republic	2004
EXIM J	Jamaica	1983
FINNVERA	Finland	1964
GIEK	Norway	1951
HKEC	Hong Kong SAR, China	1969
KSURE	Korea, Rep. of	1977
MEXIM	Malaysia	1985
NEXI	Japan	1970
ONDD	Belgium	1954
OPIC	United States	1974
SACE	Italy	1959
SERV	Switzerland	1956
SID	Slovenia	1998
SINOSURE	China	1996
SLECIC	Sri Lanka	1984
TEBC	Taiwan, China	1996
THAI EXIMBANK	Thailand	2003
TURK EXIMBANK	Turkey	1992
US EXIMBANK	United States	1962

Company	Country	Year joined
Private		
ATRADIUS[a]	Netherlands	1953
CGIC	South Africa	1958
CHARTIS	United States	1999
COFACE[a]	France	1948
COSEC[a]	Portugal	1977
ECICS	Singapore	1979
EH GERMANY[a]	Germany	1953
FCIA	United States	1963
HISCOX	Bermuda	2008
OEKB[a]	Austria	1955
PWC[a]	Germany	1974
SBCE[a]	Brazil	2001
SOVEREIGN	Bermuda	2001
ZURICH	United States	2001
Multilateral		
ICIEC	Multilateral	2007
MIGA	Multilateral	1992

a *Some medium- or long-term export credit insurance or investment insurance or both provided on account of the state.*

Appendix 9 Berne Union and Prague Club Members (cont'd)

Table A9.2 Prague Club members

Company	Country	Year joined
Public		
AOFI	Serbia	2007
BAEZ	Bulgaria	1997
BECI	Botswana	2005
ECGA	Oman	2000
ECGE	Egypt, Arab Rep.	2003
ECIC SA	South Africa	2002
ECIE	United Arab Emirates	2009
EGAP	Czech Republic	1993
EGFI	Iran, Islamic Rep. of	1999
EXIM R	Romania	1993
EXIMBANKA SR	Slovak Republic	1993
EXIMGARANT	Belarus	1999
HBOR	Croatia	1997
IGA	Bosnia and Herzegovina	1999
JLGC	Jordan	2001
KECIC	Kazakhstan	2004
KREDEX	Estonia	1999
KUKE	Poland	1993
MBDP	Macedonia, FYR	1999
MEHIB	Hungary	1993
NAIFE	Sudan	2007
NZECO	New Zealand	2010
PHILEXIM	Philippines	1997
SEP	Saudi Arabia	2000
SID	Slovenia	1993
THAI EXIMBANK	Thailand	1997
UKREXIMBANK	Ukraine	2008
UZBEKINVEST	Uzbekistan	1996
VNESHECONOMBANK	Russian Federation	2008

Company	Country	Year joined
Private		
LCI	Lebanon	2009
Multilateral		
ATI	Multilateral	2002
DHAMAN	Multilateral	2000
ICIEC	Multilateral	2001